Breaking Boundaries: Rethinking
Gender Roles in Healthcare

# Contents

I – Introduction ................................................................................................................ 1
   1 – Approach ............................................................................................................. 1
   2 – Scope .................................................................................................................. 2
   3 – Sources ............................................................................................................... 3
   4 - Summary of Chapters ......................................................................................... 5
   5 – Review of Secondary Literature ......................................................................... 7
II – The Nature of Roman Medicine ............................................................................. 13
   1 – Introduction ..................................................................................................... 13
   2 – Medicine as a Domestic Activity ..................................................................... 13
   3 – The Importance of Delivery ............................................................................. 17
   4 – Genders in Professional Medicine ................................................................... 21
   5 – Conclusions ...................................................................................................... 25
III - Medicine, Women and Society ............................................................................. 27
   1 – Introduction ..................................................................................................... 27
   2 – Changes in Female Healers Through Time ...................................................... 27
   3 – The Status of Female Physicians ..................................................................... 31
   4 – Trends in Medical Treatment .......................................................................... 35
   5 - What Female Physicians Did Not Do ............................................................... 39
   6 - Conclusions ...................................................................................................... 40
IV - Understanding Healing ......................................................................................... 42
   1 – Introduction ..................................................................................................... 42
   2 - Background of methods ................................................................................... 42
   3 - The 'Setting' of Medicine ................................................................................. 45
   4 - The 'Set' of Medical Treatments ...................................................................... 46
   5 – Understanding the Language of Medicine ..................................................... 48
   6 – Establishing the Power of Treatments ............................................................ 49
   7 – How Romans Reduced the Danger of Medicines ........................................... 52
   8 – Conclusions ...................................................................................................... 54
V – Conclusions ............................................................................................................ 56
Bibliography ................................................................................................................. 61
Appendix 1 – Roman Remedies Surveyed .................................................................. 67

# Summary

Breaking Boundaries: Rethinking Gender Roles in Healthcare" is an eye-opening and thought-provoking exploration of the intersection between gender roles and the healthcare industry. This compelling book delves deep into the complex ways in which gender expectations and stereotypes have influenced and continue to shape healthcare delivery and outcomes.

Through a multidisciplinary lens, "Breaking Boundaries" challenges conventional notions of gender in healthcare, offering a comprehensive analysis of how societal norms impact medical practices, patient experiences, and the overall health and well-being of individuals. It uncovers the historical context of gender disparities in healthcare and examines their contemporary manifestations.

Readers will gain valuable insights into the ways in which gender bias, discrimination, and inequities affect both healthcare professionals and patients. The book highlights the experiences of healthcare providers breaking free from traditional gender roles and the impact of their actions on patient care.

"Breaking Boundaries" also explores the innovative strategies and approaches that are reshaping the healthcare landscape to be more inclusive and gender-aware. It examines the importance of diversity in the healthcare workforce and the need for gender-sensitive policies and practices.

This book is a vital resource for healthcare professionals, policymakers, educators, and anyone interested in fostering a more equitable and responsive healthcare system. "Breaking Boundaries" empowers readers to challenge preconceived notions, advocate for gender equality in healthcare, and ultimately contribute to a more inclusive and effective healthcare environment for all.

# I – Introduction

## 1 – Approach

My thesis employs two contemporary methodological approaches: social and cultural history. Social history emphasises understanding the function of society through the investigation of social relationships. In contrast cultural history attempts to understand how people applied meaning to people and objects in an attempt to understand their culture.

The approach principally used in chapters one and two is that of social history. Chapter two investigates to what extent healing can be seen as part of the female domestic role. This enquiry aims to identify the social relationship between genders in Roman society and the nature of the domestic space within which social relations occurred. Chapter three utilises the practice of healing as evidence to understand women's status within society more generally. This approach influences the sources I have used and the relative significance of these various sources. Sources which refer to medicine but were not written by professional male physicians are extremely valuable.[1] Additionally my investigation seeks to overcome the distinction between professional and non-professional healers which is a modern categorisation wrongfully applied to the Roman world.[2]

Chapter four, in contrast, uses the information gathered in sections one and two and interprets it using a cultural historical lens with a view to recreating the 'meanings' associated with different pharmaceuticals. Specifically it will attempt to understand which pharmaceuticals and treatments were seen as more powerful or significant in the Roman world. To accomplish this it will consider what substances could be administered and treatments could be performed by men and women respectively and, based on our understanding of social relationships, theorise what status or significance a Roman may associate with such a treatment. This component of the study will be

---

[1] In the context of this work 'physician' refers to a trained healer working in general medicine or midwifery.
[2] In the context of this work 'professional' refers to those performing a task as an occupation regardless of training, as well as those who identify themselves with such an occupation. 'Healer' refers to someone involved in some aspect of medical treatment whether professional or not, regardless of their area of specialisation.

based on modern anthropological studies which highlight the interaction between the meaning associated with a treatment and its effectiveness.[3]

Additionally my investigation will be shaped by gender studies. Gender studies highlight the manner in which gender roles are understood and created by a society. It then applies this understanding to better comprehend how different genders interacted and how a society functioned.[4] Broadly speaking my enquiry will attempt to understand the relationship between gender and Roman healing. Healing is, however, a fundamentally cultural process which is greatly influenced by a patient's 'relationship' to the treatment and healer.[5] As such I will consider the cultural construction of gender and healing.

## 2 – Scope

The time period for my study is the first two dynasties of the Roman Empire: from the accession of Augustus in 27 BC to the end of the Flavian Dynasty with the death of Domitian in AD 96. This time period was a time of great change in medicine as within this range we see the decline of traditional Roman healing and the slow adoption of Greek practices. This time period is also one in which medicine is infrequently studied. Older studies investigating Roman medicine in the later empire use the works of Galen as their main sources and more recent works explore the nature of medicine in the republican period. Of these, studies of the republican period often extend into the period of my investigation, particularly through the use of Pliny. In contrast those studying the later empire rarely differentiate between medicine before and after Galen. As one professor put the question "What Roman medicine was there before Galen?" – a telling reflection of the traditional view.

---

[3] Some anthropological works used: Moerman and Jonas (2002); Katz (1999); Lakoff and Johnson (1980); Moerman and Jonas (2002); Rivers (1927); Singer and Baer (2012); Watters (2010).
[4] Some key historical gender studies literature: Adcock (1945); Bourdillon (1988); Cameron and Kuhrt (1987); Dewitt (1920); Dingwall, et al. (2002); Ehrenreich and English (2010); Flemming (2000); Flemming (2007); Hemelrijk (2004); King (1998); King (2007); Koloski-Ostrow and Lyons (1997); Rawson (1986); Retief and Cilliers (2006).
[5] Where 'relationship' appears in inverted commas I am using it to represent the manner in which they conceive and construct the object and their relationship to it. For a fuller explanation see Rubin (2008).

In order to gain a better understanding of this period however, I have also utilised sources from beyond this period. This supplements the lack of sources which grapple with social and cultural aspects of Roman healing particularly in terms of how ordinary people practised healing. The use of sources both before and after the focus of this study creates an understanding of how medicine has changed over time. This permits a reconstruction of medical practices within the timeframe of this study. As cultural views are generally slow to change,[6] rather than being a feature which can be changed by a single event we can create a line of best fit for the changes occurring in this period. For example, if Cato suggests that Romans resisted Greek medicine whereas Galen states and shows that Greek medicine was common and popular in his own time, we can infer that this changed within the period of my study.

Most studies of ancient medicine focus on the Greek approach to healing. While the Greek approach lends itself to the intricate studies suitable for history with numerous factions and theories of medicine this has led to the Roman world being overshadowed. Further many of those who do consider the Roman world present it as simply the successor to Greek practice. My investigation will reassess the distinctiveness of Roman medicine. Although I will not exclude information from anywhere in the Roman Empire my study will aim to understand the medical traditions of Italy. This limitation is necessary as it represents a fairly unified culture. In contrast, if I were to study medicine in Greece in the Roman period, there would be no trace of traditional Italic healing which characterised the healing practices in Italy.

## 3 – Sources

In order to gain the best understanding of Roman views my investigation employs a variety of source types. Although there have been many traditional studies which limit themselves to the literary and medical sources, these represent the views of only a small fraction of the population. Furthermore

---

[6] Mead (1937:17); Monaghan and Just (2000:47-48)

they only portray the opinions of specialists or those claiming to be specialists.[7] This means that whatever social information can be pieced together from these sources is unlikely to fairly represent the views of the majority of the population.

Because the application of medicine is the central theme of such works, they tend to avoid discussion of social and cultural aspects of healing. A notable exception to this trend is Pliny who includes references to folk remedies though he often discourages their use and lacks any belief in their effectiveness.

Similarly, as many of the works which investigate ancient medicine have been written by those without a historical background, these accounts often have a lack of evidence. Such studies are typically carried out by those with a medical background and through schools of medicine rather than history.[8] The use of a broad array of source types attempts to counter this trend. Additionally, I will compare these sources to establish their accuracy and to gain a more thorough understanding. This critical approach is often also lacking in these enquiries as they often focus, usually unintentionally, on a single or limited set of sources. This is particularly evident in those who utilise Pliny and Galen.[9]

To overcome this, my work uses the fragmentary references which can be found in other forms of evidence. Some notable examples which I have used are letters, particularly those of Cicero which yield valuable insight into how healing was carried out in the family. There are also limited references in plays. Here, the most valuable date to slightly before my period, particularly the comedies of Plautus. Epigraphic sources can also be quite effective in providing information especially that not mentioned in other forms of evidence.

---

[7] In the context of this work 'specialist' refers to someone who is ascribed status through experience or training who works in a particular field.
[8] The school of medicine at the University of Wisconsin – Madison is seemingly the most prolific producer of academics investigating the history of medicine.
[9] Authors with a medical background: Cushing (1998); Hillman (2004); Jackson (1988). Authors who rely heavily on Pliny or Galen: Abbott (1911); Allbutt (1921); Jackson (1988); Majno (1975); Nutting (1907); Scarborough (1969); Scarborough (1970); Scarborough (1993).

Although the use of an array of sources is useful the literary evidence is still extremely important and forms the majority of my body of evidence. Most sources which grapple with medicine in the first century use Pliny as a major source of information. Books XX to XXIX of his *Naturalis Historiae* particularly focus on medicine. Often these enquiries become overly dependent on this text, as it is the most substantial work on this period and the Republic. Pliny's aim in this work, however, was to preserve older Roman traditions. As a result his work can convey an inaccurate view of medicine in his own period and this needs to be kept in mind when using him as a source.

Soranus' *Gynaecology* is an extremely important source for my study. Although it is slightly outside my period, the treatments in this work represent medicines we can be sure could be applied by women.[10] This is vital in order to be able to differentiate between the medicines applied by either male or female physicians. Although for non-professional domestic healers we must rely on fragmentary sources to gain information, Soranus still provides great insight. I then compare sources that establish the roles of female healers with the other more general sources to differentiate between various treatments.

Two other sources are very useful in understanding medicine in this period: firstly the work of Dioscorides and secondly that of Scribonius. Both of these medical authors wrote within the period of my study and so provide valuable information on medicines at the time. Being medical writers they offer limited understanding of cultural aspects.

Although archaeological evidence is often prized in history for its ability to give an insight into culture it does not form a major component of my study. This is principally as the evidence it provides mostly relates to particular types of healing such as surgery which leave material remains.. Also while study of the buildings in which healing took place for its archaeological data is insightful, these are difficult to identify as healing was usually carried out in a home or in movable shops.

## 4 - Summary of Chapters

---

[10] Soranus, *Gynecology*, 1.4.

Chapter II – "The Nature of Roman Medicine" illustrates that healing was closely associated with the domestic role. It achieves this by using references which discuss healing being carried out in the home without the need for a professional physician. I then consider the issue of whether the home can be seen as an environment controlled by the *paterfamilias* or by women. Based on the letters of Cicero and other sources we see that healing must often have been the responsibility of a woman. Inscriptional evidence also shows that healing was considered a valuable domestic skill for a woman and so suggests that it was part of their duties.

Chapter III – "Medicine, Women and Society" considers the implications of a women administering medical care in the ancient world. It establishes that this must represent a reversal from the higher status usually held by men. This is considered in conjunction with the implications of slaves performing a similar task to create a comparison. Thus it furthers our understanding of the status of women in Roman society.

Chapter IV – "Understanding Healing" reconstructs how Romans 'relate' to various pharmaceuticals and treatments. It accomplishes this by integrating anthropological research to justify the association between a patients 'relationship' to the treatment and the practices which surround it. In this case the main practice which is discussed is the distinction between medicines which can be applied by different genders, although other rituals associated with medical treatments will be used to justify the reconstruction of a treatment's significance. This chapter will thus allow for an understanding of how different pharmaceuticals were valued relative to one another in Roman society.

Chapter V – "Conclusions" will summarise the work and clarify the connections between gender roles and healing in Roman Italy by utilizing the information gained from the previous chapters. This chapter will also provide suggested areas of further study to broaden our knowledge of gender roles and healing.

# 5 – Review of Secondary Literature

This review will provide a summary of the relevant modern literature related to the study of gender and Roman medicine. It will also mention other key scholars important to my particular study. It will span from Nutting in 1907 to the present. This will both provide the reader with an understanding of this work's context and enrich their understanding of the need and significance of the current study.

There have been numerous major works which have investigated medicine in the Roman world. Likely the most influential work in this field is T. C. Allbutt's *Greek Medicine in Rome*, 1921, which was an expansion on his earlier *Fitzpatrick Lectures*, 1909. As its title suggests Allbutt believed that Roman medicine was entirely the result of Greek influences. This led to this becoming the accepted view in the academic community and has remained a common view through to recent times. Allbutt's work also excluded discussion of women and presented domestic medicine as being principally the responsibility of the *paterfamilias*. So while this work resulted in many of the fallacies which my work tries to reassess it is thus very important in gaining an understanding from where these views came.

J. Scarborough's *Roman Medicine*, 1969, provides a comprehensive insight into Roman healing with a particular emphasis on earlier periods. Scarborough mostly utilises Pliny as a source of information. Due to the thorough nature of Pliny's work this leads Scarborough to focus on the supernatural and folk aspects of Roman healing. This contrasts with the rational and scientific methods employed by the Greeks and usually fore fronted in the modern scholarship. He expands and strengthens this position based on other archaeological sources from religious contexts. He highlights that healing often appeared to occur in religious contexts and in Pliny's works many medical treatments had associated spells or rituals needed to make the treatment function. This relates to the distinction of biomedicine from traditional healing as advocated in early anthropologists such as Rivers. His work notably surpasses Allbutt's in understanding the social position of physicians in society and the status of both professional and nonprofessional healers.

The work of M. A. Nutting and her *A History of Nursing*, in 1907, is also important to modern scholarship. This massive work which covers nursing from the Greek world through to the contemporary was doubtlessly avant-garde in considering the newly created discipline of nursing and by extension female healers. Her work still contains many useful insights into nursing in the ancient world. Her summary of how rights and status were given both to physicians and nurses is particularly clear and useful. Nutting however reinforced the view that female doctors were uncommon and that women would only work as nurses in various capacities. Since, after much debate, a decision had been reached that nurses required formal training to successfully do their job, Nutting also promotes that women in the ancient world received some sort of formal training. While this is possibly an accurate assessment she does not contextualize this training by comparing it to the minimal training male physicians received. The issue of medical training was later addressed in I. E. Drabkin's *On Medical Education in Greece and Rome*, 1944, which establishes that medical knowledge was most often transferred via an apprenticeship rather than academic means.

R. Jackson, in 1988, also compiled a work of substantial scope however this was still of small size and so only provides a good overview to medicine in the empire. His work does cover an impressive amount of information and has been regularly cited in other works. He however follows Allbutt in suggesting that Roman medicine was principally a successor to Greek practises. He also spends little time discussing the involvement of any women and where such mention is made he gives them little credibility as professional physicians. He presents women almost exclusively as midwives and believes that they were certainly only used in treating other women. Such a view contrasts with that of Retief and Cilliers below who establish that female healers were well respected in society and so suggest that they could also treat other members of their communities. Jackson is also highly dependent on literary sources making no meaningful use of other forms of evidence. In my thesis I will use a broader range of sources to prevent such limitations.

In contrast to Allbutt and Jackson, D.C. A. Hillman in his 2004 investigation of republican medicine presents a distinctly Roman medical system which, although eventually accepting of Greek medicine, had a different view of what disease was and how it was to be treated. Although Jackson had emphasised that pre-Greek medicine in Italy was simplistic Hillman showed that treatments required great domestic expertise and related specifically to Italy's geographic and social context. He promotes the view that each family would mostly be responsible for their own healing and that to achieve this they would use a traditional knowledge of drug lore specific to the medicaments available in their area. This is in contrast to Roman medicine in later times in which medicine became more formal and universal in relation to the treatments they would prescribe. He also used a broader array of sources drawing particularly on plays, agricultural manuals and letters. This allowed him to gain a better understanding of how the average person related to medicine rather than the select few who wrote medical works. Hillman also takes great care to differentiate between urban and rural pharmacy emphasising that the approaches in the republic were quite distinct, while those in the cities had begun to adopt the Greek approach those in the country retained closer links between religion and healing and tended to perform treatments using local knowledge rather than 'professionally' trained doctors.

Bailey, in her investigation into Roman domestic medicine (2012), establishes that the role of women was of great importance in the medical system overall. She clearly establishes that medicine is a domestic activity and that this aspect of the domestic space was the responsibility of women rather than the *paterfamilias* as suggested by Allbutt. In her enquiry Bailey, like Hillman, uses a greater variety of sources giving additional authority to her investigation. Bailey also touches on the issue of distinction between professional and non-professional medicine. She hypothesises the presence of informal 'women's networks' and places the origin of this practice in $5^{th}$ century Greece. Her understanding of these networks was largely based on artistic materials which led her to propose the continued coexistence of these women's networks alongside formal female healers in the empire. As her investigation seeks to understand the domestic aspects of healing she considers how often external professional medicine must be used and the status of the individuals providing this service. This is important to understand when researching domestic medicine or the roles of women.

The most substantial work which investigated women in the Roman world was R. Flemming. Her work of 2000, while well received, still tends to present women as only treating their own gender and in roles that were seen as less significant than their male counterparts. This contrasts with the views of Bailey and her interpretation of medical women in the professional sphere. Additionally it disregards the contribution of Hillman in emphasising the complex advanced knowledge of the nonprofessional Roman healer. Her work skilfully utilises nearly all written sources in order to gain a fuller understanding. This included extracting fragmentary information from later sources.

To understand gender roles in healing one must also be familiar with family structure and although Allbutt gives some suggestions on these matters it is useful to consult specialist works. To this end B. Rawson's work *The Roman Family*, 1986, is invaluable in understanding the traditional interpretation of family structure. Although accurate in most circumstances it is established by Bailey that the control exerted by the *paterfamilias* on the family was not direct but theoretical and that practical interactions with the family must be in another's control.

Many sources which consider women and their relationship to healing focus principally on the Greek world. This again is likely a result of Allbutt's approach. F. P. Retief and L. Cilliers 2006 article 'The Healing Hand: the role of women in Greco-Roman medicine' is such an example. This work views Roman medicine as a result of Greek approaches and understanding. Their work is however valuable apart from this tendency and is thus useful in tracking Greek influences. This work also emphasises that female healers were well respected in ancient classical communities and treated equivalent to their male counterparts.

W. Jashemski's text *A Pompeian Herbal*, 1999 is useful in its discussion of the environmental conditions in Italy. Additionally it clearly sets out particular pharmaceuticals, pairs them to key references in the ancient texts and discusses likely ancient uses for the plant. It supports these interpretations based on ethnographic information gathered during the author's stay in Pompeii related to how modern people use these substances. This method is reflective of the tendency in scholars such as Hillman and ancient works, particularly Pliny, to emphasise the treatments themselves rather than social aspects or diagnoses.

The works of V. Nutton active from 1977 to the present, point out that Pliny is overused in the reconstruction of Roman medicine and doing this has led to many errors. For this reason his works aim to utilise other sources to give a clearer picture of medicine. This is in contrast to earlier scholarship such as Allbutt and Scarborough who rely heavily on Pliny. Nutton does however hold to the view that Roman Medicine was eventually surpassed and overshadowed by the Greek approach. This is foreshadowed in the work of Pliny which aimed to resist this change. This view however is also supported by Galen who writes in the model of the Greek approach to medicine.

Mention must be made of the many articles published in the 1993 Aufstieg und Niedergang der Römischen Welt which dealt specifically with Roman medicine. Notably Scarborough's article, Roman Medicine to Galen investigates traditional forms of Roman medicine and its associations with religion and magic. It also considers the influence of Greek medicine on the development of Roman methods. Jackson also contributed an article, *Roman Medicine: The Practitioners and their Practices*, which, like Bailey, contrasts public and private physicians. Although he is again dependent on written sources the argument is well considered and argued. Most substantially, Nutton too published an article in which he again confronts the usefulness of Pliny as a source, on this occasion considering whether Greek and Roman medicine were as closely related as Pliny presents. In doing this he not only confronts Pliny but also the copious scholars who have followed this perspective.

My investigation will also attempt some cultural reconstruction of the Roman medical system. M. Singer and H. Baer's *Introduction to Medical Anthropology*, 2000, is a valuable source for outlining the methods and aims of such an enquiry. Medical anthropology aims to understand the experience of sickness as a result of illness (personal experience) and disease (the way a culture categorises such illnesses). While diseases may be relatively easy to identify and understand in first century Rome, how the sick actually experienced them is more challenging to interpret. I utilise a variety of evidence to reconstruct the treatment experience of the sick in different situations. While this is not as useful as personal testimony it still provides some insight into sickness in the Roman world. This being an anthropological text, however, does not assist with the collection of data or propose how to work with limited sources of information such as those available in ancient history.

*Medicine, Magic and Religion* by W. H. R. Rivers, 1927, has traditionally been regarded as the foundational work of medical anthropology. While he established medicine within the sphere of anthropology and thus culture, he separates western biomedicine from the folk, 'ethnomedicine' which he investigates and claims is free from cultural influences. This naive idea has been strongly opposed by most recent work in anthropology such as P. Katz, 1999 D. Moerman and W. Jonas, 2002 who all highlight the ritual and cultural aspects within our own medical system. So while the Roman approach to medicine may, as is almost universally agreed, focus heavily on simply applying the correct medicine for the correct symptom there is still valuable culture to be understood.

It is clear from these enquiries that women did have some involvement in medicine, although the precise form of this involvement is debated. A full continuum appears between those who believe women were scarcely involved as nurses to those who promote that they were equal to their male counterparts. Additionally most works suggest that Roman medicine focused on the practicalities of treatment rather than theory. This approach has often been mirrored in the secondary scholarship leading to a disregard of the social and cultural aspects of healing. A further debate arises between those who position domestic healing with the *paterfamilias* such as Allbutt and those who believe that this was part of the female role such as Bailey.

# II – The Nature of Roman Medicine

## 1 – Introduction

To get a proper understanding of gender roles in medicine in Roman society I will begin by examining to what extent healing can be seen as part of domestic responsibilities. This discussion will have two components: it will begin by analysing medicine as a domestic or professional activity, and will then continue by examining whether this distinction can be seen as significant. This chapter will incorporate both a detailed discussion of Roman and contemporary views with critical references to both the ancient and modern scholarship.

## 2 – Medicine as a Domestic Activity

In first century Rome, in contrast to the modern west, medicine was much more commonly carried out in the home without the intervention of a medical physician. Although there were expert physicians in Rome in this period, these appear to have been used only as a last resort.

For the most part the evidence suggests that the primary medical practitioner in the Roman world was the *paterfamilias*[11]. The medical texts of Celsus aim to assist the understanding of a *paterfamilias* to provide appropriate care to his family. The most striking evidence for this is his differentiation between remedies that would be 'on hand' and those which were used by specialists.[12] This would have been unnecessary if his audience were trained physicians having access to such obscure remedies and who would likely already be familiar with their use.[13] His use of indirect forms of address also suggests that he was informing *patresfamilias* rather than instructing physicians.[14]

---

[11] This is also the standard view adopted by modern scholarship beginning with Allbutt (1909). See too Bailey (2012); Jackson (1988) c.f. Hillman (2004:22-33): 'Practitioner' (or 'medical practitioner') is one involved in healing with some formal or informal training which thus ascribes them a position of authority
[12] Celsus, *De Medicina*, II. 33. 1-4.
[13] Bailey (2012:29).
[14] Pinkster (1992:520).

Pliny's *Naturalis Historiae* likewise seems addressed to the *paterfamilias*. The sizable scope of his investigations would have been unnecessary if his text was directed towards professional physicians. It functions more as an instructive encyclopaedia, suitable for the educated public.[15] Pliny also expresses hostility towards professional physicians, which indicates that these men were not his main target audience.[16] These writings, although before the period of this study, must reflect the traditional Roman view and have undoubtedly contributed to the continuation of this belief among modern studies.[17]

Although these sources illustrate that, in the Republic, medicine was commonly practiced in the domestic space, they also show that this had become less common by the time of their creation. One of Pliny's aims in writing the *NH* was to record native Roman medical traditions in order to preserve them for the future.[18] This illustrates that professional medicine, particularly that of the Greeks, was gaining popularity to the detriment of the Roman tradition. This trend continued and so reduced the practice of domestic medicine.[19]

We now turn to the role of the *patresfamilias* in contrast to women in the Roman household. Although the *paterfamilias* was certainly the theoretical and legal head of the Roman family, his involvement in the domestic space would not have been as direct as his wife.[20] This is illustrated by the difference in gender associations with either the domestic or public spheres. This separation is seen in ancient works such as Columella as well as made clear in modern studies.[21] The particular involvement of the *paterfamilias* in medicine is well illustrated in the letters of Cicero to his family.[22] In these, although he takes an interest in the wellbeing of those under his legal care, he is clearly not in a position to provide direct assistance. He does give suggestions and even advises the use of professional physicians such as in letter 41 to his slave Tiro where he states *"Medico mercedis*

---

[15] Flemming (2000:59).
[16] Pliny, *Naturalis Historiae*, XXIX. 5.
[17] Pliny's writings aimed to preserve older Roman traditions see Bailey (2012:21)
[18] Bailey (2012:21).
[19] Jackson (1988:12).
[20] Scullard (2009:338-339)
[21] Columella, *De Re Rustica,* 12. praef. 1-8 ; Hemelrijk (2004:188).
[22] Cicero, *Epistulae ad Familiares,* 6.14.4; Cicero, *Epistulae ad Familiares,* 155.14.7.

*quantum poscet promitti iubeto"*.[23] These letters (of n.21 and 22) show that although it is his responsibility to be concerned about the health of his family, he is often not available to provide support and so treatments must often have been rendered by others. In some cases, such as that of Tiro, this would be a professional physician, while in others it would be another member of the household, especially the mother.[24]

The role of being an adviser appears to more accurately represent the role of the *bonus paterfamilias*. This interpretation of their involvement is also supported by the medical encyclopaedias written for their use.[25] While an amateur may feel confident to apply some simple remedies, these encyclopaedias do not give enough details on complex medicines for a reader to apply them safely. Instead, the inclusion of these dangerous treatments should be viewed as background information for a *paterfamilias* to employ when selecting an appropriate professional.[26] Such information may have been used both to judge a physician's competency, based on knowledge of such treatments, and to make a correct diagnosis so that the appropriate specialist is selected for the illness.[27]

In contrast to the modern world there were no qualifications for physicians and it was important that someone be able to judge the competence of a practitioner.[28] To do this accurately someone in the family needed to stay informed about common medical treatments. It was also important to stay appraised of well-known physicians so that one did not hire an 'oafish quack' as commonly presented in plays, poems and other literary works.[29]

Another core factor which must have influenced medicine as a domestic activity was to what extent private individuals would have been able to source medicinal substances.[30] The mineral treatments

---

[23] Cicero, *Epistulae ad Familiares,* 41.26.14. 'Give orders for the doctor to be promised whatever fee he asks.'
[24] Bailey (2012:63).
[25] Bailey (2012:4).
[26] Flemming (2000:59).
[27] Jackson (1988:32).
[28] Bailey (2012:46f.).
[29] e.g. Plautus, *Menaechmi,* 950.
[30] The public displays of the *marsus* suggest that they sold their remedies to the general public rather than merely physicians. See Nutton (1985:139).

as discussed by Celsus would not have been accessible to the general population and so, if a disease required a mineral treatment, it could not be carried out in the home. In contrast most plant based medicines would have been accessible from dedicated shops in markets and so these treatments could likely be used by laymen in a domestic environment.[31]

There is strong evidence that women did provide practical medical assistance both within the period of this study and earlier. This evidence comes from the agricultural manuals in relation to the care of the rural household and particularly the slaves.[32] The instructions suggest that it is the responsibility of the wife of the slave master to care for the slaves and maintain a healing room and supplies.[33] This proves that women could be trusted with such tasks and assume a position of authority over men. This example however is quite narrow, and there are numerous factors which may explain this away as non-standard. Firstly, the patients in this situation were slaves and so perhaps the same social rules did not apply.[34] In this case though the woman, too, was a slave and so the practitioner and patient, being on an equal social standing would be subject to their normal gender roles.[35] Secondly, it could be identified that the woman herself being a slave is still subject to the control of her own master. This is a sound objection except that this is a description of a large estate where the owner was unlikely to be heavily involved with the practical operation of the property. Finally we can say that this represents a rural environment in which access to professional physicians would be limited. Although this does explain the need to keep supplies for more complex medical treatments it does not alter the fact that the application of these substances was left to a woman, albeit one of higher status, rather than a man. From this it is clear that at least in a rural context women were trusted and made the responsible parties for the administration of medical treatments as well as the acquisition of relevant supplies and treatment spaces.

The use of household items associated with women is also an indication that healing often fell within the scope of the female domestic role. The use of wool with various other ingredients, as is often

---

[31] Nutton (1985:140).
[32] Such as Cato, *De Agricultura*, ; Columella, *De Re Rustica*,
[33] Columella, *De Re Rustica*, XII. 3. 7.
[34] See Cato's instructions on how the slaves should be treated compared to cattle. Cato, *De Agricultura*, V. 6.
[35] Bailey (2012:115).

suggested by Pliny, is an example of using a common domestic item in a medicinal way.[36] The strong associations of wool with women would suggest that such treatments may well have been carried out by the female members of the house or at least that they would have been involved in the preparation and acquisition of supplies.[37] This relates to the access of household members to supplies which will be discussed more thoroughly below.

## 3 – The Importance of Delivery

Although much of scholarship agrees that women were involved in the practicalities of the healing process, many of these studies regard this as insignificant. Such enquiries suggest that Roman society prized only the remedies themselves without any concern for the person who delivered them.[38] While many Roman writers professed this view, I will argue that this position does not reflect the realities of Roman medical treatment by utilizing a broader range of sources and by cross-cultural comparisons of medical systems.

Historians such as Jackson emphasise that, in the republic, the individual delivering a treatment could be anyone and that this was of no real importance. He ascribes this to the importance of religion in traditional Italic remedies that led to them placing no importance on the diagnosis or prognosis of a disease, it not being a human concern.[39] This resulted in an assortment of treatments which only aimed to alleviate the visible symptoms.[40] This began to change after the interaction with rationalist Greek models of medicine.[41]

The view of modern scholarship has been greatly affected by ancient works such as Pliny, who structured his work to emphasise substances themselves rather than practitioners. This evidence has been employed by scholars such as Hillman and Bailey to illustrate that medicinal substances were

---

[36] Pliny, *Naturalis Historiae*, XXIX. 9. 29.
[37] Dewitt (1920:222); Poblome (2004:492).
[38] Majno (1975:339); Allbutt (1921:24); Scarborough (1993:13); Bailey (2012:16f.) c.f. Pliny, *Naturalis Historiae*, 29.8.15-16.
[39] Jackson (1988:11).
[40] Allbutt (1921:25); Hillman (2004:22).
[41] Jackson (1988:14).

seen as the most significant aspect of Roman healing.[42] It seems, however, that this interpretation is overstretched. Pliny, in writing his natural history, presented more than merely a medical text. His aim was to present what was known of the natural world in an encyclopaedic format; he thus sequenced his work to highlight objects of the natural world.[43] For this reason his work should not be used to give insight into the Roman psyche.

Other ancient sources too, such as Celsus, pay little attention to social aspects of medicine. Although he places greater emphasis on the diseases as well as merely the treatments, he still places little emphasis on who administers a treatment.[44] Celsus' work seems to move slightly closer to the Greek model encouraging the use of *dietetics* and placing some importance on the diseases.[45] His work also separates the substances that would be on hand and the substances that are more professional.[46] This shows that his work is directed at the non-expert and that they were expected to apply many of these treatments themselves.

Sources such as Pliny also state that it was the remedies which were significant rather than the physician, stating *non rem antiqui damnabant, sed artem*.[47] Rather than taking these at face value we should instead consider the purpose of these texts. There would be no purpose in stating that the remedies, rather than the physician, should be the significant aspect if this was already the case. This would suggest that although being concerned only with the pharmaceuticals was viewed as the ideal, it was not the reality. So such accounts, far from suggesting that the Roman concern was only with the substances, indicates that many Romans were interested in the reputation and renown of the healer.

It is possible that this type of statement represents a divide present in Roman society between the literate elite and the lower classes. It is clear that these writers believed that an objective approach

---

[42] Hillman (2004:22); Bailey (2012).
[43] Murphy (2004).
[44] Celsus, *De Medicina,* book III; Bailey (2012:35-36).
[45] Celsus, *De Medicina,* praef. 9.
[46] Celsus, *De Medicina,* II. 33.1-4.
[47] Pliny, *Naturalis Historiae,* XXIX. 8It was not medicine itself that the forefathers condemned, but medicine as a profession… chiefly because they refused to pay fees to profiteers in order to save their own lives.

based on the medicinals used was the ideal but, having felt the need to write it, this must not have been the case. This suggests that the mainstream of the Roman people did not accept this rationalist view.

Similarly there was a distinction between urban and rural medical treatment. Rural medicine tended to be more traditional than urban treatments.[48] For this reason the medical approaches used in the early empire seemed to differ substantially between the practices in the country and in the city. This distinction, of course, also affected the perception of women and their role in healing. Rural medicine continued to place greater significance on the substances and the gods thus giving little credit to the person who prepared and administered the drugs.[49] This likely meant that it was more often the role of a woman to prepare and deliver these than a physician.

Rural pharmacy was also more likely to use local knowledge of native pharmaceutical plants than those in the city. As remains the case, those who grow up in an area close to nature have a thorough knowledge of these items, and so in the case of medicine would be more likely to use them. Although it has been argued by Scarborough that all Romans would have had considerable knowledge of flora and fauna, this would undoubtedly have been better amongst those who lived in the country.[50] Furthermore a rural environment would allow for easier access to medicinals which may also have encouraged a tendency for medicine to be carried out by women in a domestic environment.

Finally the access to physicians would have been much less in a rural environment. While many cities had paid physicians for their populations, in a rural area doctors would likely be only sporadically available.[51] Again this shows that the role of women and domestic healing was more significant in the country.

---

[48] Hillman (2004:65); Bailey (2012:82).
[49] Bailey (2012:86-87).
[50] Scarborough (1986:60).
[51] See surgeons in Mariani-Costantini, et al. (2000).

Rural medicine also tended to employ more magical and religious aspects of healing.[52] Magic was significant in traditional italic folk medicine and there is evidence that this continued to varying degrees both in the city and country. Soranus warns *obstetrices* not to engage with superstition. This suggests that the practice of magical and religious healing continued through to at least the second century. Adcock expressed the view that this illustrates a continuation of folk healing.[53] Such healing practices would seemingly encourage the role of women as they were seen as suitable to perform magic and be involved with religion.

In Greek medicine we see quite a different view of the aims of medicine which, by the early empire, were likely having an influence on Roman approaches. Greek medicine valued diagnosis and prognosis, a point often parodied by Roman authors.[54] For this reason the skill, training and indeed 'school' of the physician were held to be of great importance.[55] As Greek and Roman cultures began to interact more readily we could expect that the Romans may, too, begin to prize skilled and professionally trained physicians. More practically, with the expansion of Roman borders, their society would have been in contact with the major medical training centres such as Alexandria whose medical schools flourished under the Ptolemies.[56]

It would be surprising if the Romans placed little to no significance on the treating professional as this would seem to ignore an aspect of human physiology namely the 'meaning response'.[57] From the study of Moerman and Jonas it is clear that the behaviour and status of a medical practitioner is of great significance to the meaning for the patient and so the likely effectiveness of any treatments.[58] This would in fact have been even more significant in the ancient Roman world as few of their treatments had actual medicinal benefits.[59] Even if the population did not know it consciously, the

---

[52] Pliny, *Naturalis Historiae*, 30. 1-2; Adcock (1945:10).
[53] Adcock (1945:10).
[54] Plautus, *Menaechmi*, 950.
[55] Jackson (1988:15f.); Herodotus, ἱστορία, II. 84.
[56] Jackson (1988:14).
[57] Commonly called the placebo effect however this is shown to be an incorrect term by Moerman and Jonas (2002:471) and here I have followed their renaming.
[58] Moerman and Jonas (2002:473).
[59] Nutton (1986:55-56).

people who delivered medical treatments were a vital part of the healing process and so, if these healers could be women, it suggests that they held some authority in these matters.

## 4 – Genders in Professional Medicine

We now turn to a consideration of gender roles amongst professional healers. The healers who will be discussed can be defined by a variety of terms, namely: *medici* (or *medicae*) (the general physicians), *obstetrices* (midwives), *iatraliptae* (medical trainers or attendants) and *herbarii* (herbalists; dealers in medical materials) these terms mostly differentiated between different approaches and specialisations in medicine.[60] The main practitioners who will be discussed in this section are *medici*, the general doctors, and *obstetrices,* the gynaecologists/midwives.

As we have seen above women were clearly involved in the domestic use of medicine. They also often worked in some of the positions listed above.

The most obvious field in which women worked to provide medical aid was midwifery. Women in this occupation are very commonly attested through written texts as well as from art.[61] Although the primary purpose of this role was assisting with the delivery of children, their actual activities seemed to be much broader.

These women treated most of the 'women's diseases' like hysteria in addition to their basic birthing role.[62] They also provided treatment for abortion or contraception as later writings on the subject, such as Metrodora, show.[63] These medical texts written by women are an invaluable source into understanding the realities of women in such roles. Most of the other ancient texts written about female health encourage patients to seek out the assistance of male physicians rather than female ones who were seen to be incompetent.

---

[60] Flemming (2000:33).
[61] Rawson (2003:101-102); Lawton (2007:42).
[62] Flemming (2000:264-266)See Galen, *De Praegnotione ad Epigenem,* 8.
[63] Retief and Cilliers (2006:173) see also. Soranus, *Gynecology,* I. 65; Hillman (2008:50).

This sentiment is of great interest, it is likely a manifestation of cultural views which seek to restrict situations where the status of a *paterfamilias* may be undermined by a woman who, by way of being hired for the purpose, is ascribed with greater knowledge than the head of the family. This consequently furthers the position that the person delivering treatment did have cultural importance and was an important aspect of Roman healing.

Such a statement relating to the competence or otherwise of female healers leads us to consider the comparative training of male versus female healers. Certainly most females working as midwives would likely be doing so without any or at best little formal training.[64] This is stated in ancient sources such as Pliny and is supported by the regular mention of the apparent incompetence of these women.[65] There is a dispute in modern academia as to whether female healers had access to formal training. Nutton, Hillman and Bailey believe that women had no access to formal training whereas Jackson argues the opposite. Flemming separates the titles for different female healers and thus argues that some of these had access to formal training while others did not. Although this may appear to suggest that female healers were 'unprofessional' it is unlikely that many of the male physicians would have received more extensive training. The authority of a doctor in the Roman world could only be judged based on his reputation and no other system existed to qualify a medical professional.[66] This of course led to poor quality standards in terms of physicians leading to their often bad reputation in comedy and statements in literature such as *"discunt periculis nostris et experimenta per mortes agunt, medicoque tantum hominem occidisse inpunitas summa est"*.[67]

While it was expected that a doctor would complete a multi-year apprenticeship this level of training may easily have been matched by women albeit in a less formal setting.[68] This would suggest that the distinction drawn between women who received formal training and those who are often referred to by modern scholarship as part of a women's network, is a fabrication of modern views on training.

---

[64] Nutton (2004:197).
[65] Pliny, *Naturalis Historiae,* XXV. V. 9-10.
[66] Drabkin (1944:337); Flemming (2000:45-46)
[67] Pliny, *Naturalis Historiae,* XXIX. 8. 18.They become acquainted with knowledge from our dangers and conduct experiments through our deaths. Only a physician may kill a man with complete impunity.
[68] Flemming (2007:261); Flemming (2000:59-61); Drabkin (1944).

Indeed the existence of any women involved in medicine in apparent violation of Roman culture suggests that at least some of these practitioners must have been skilled and thus appropriately 'trained' to make their services more desirable than their male counterparts.

There is also copious evidence that women were employed as general physicians. Firstly there are many references in inscriptions to *medica* which would suggest this. Some of these, such as CIL VI 7581, show that women were functioning as professional doctors. This inscription reads

*deae sanctae meae / Primillae medicae / L Vibi Melitonis f(iliae) / vixit annis xxxxiiii / ex eis cum L Cocceio / Apthoro xxx sine querella fecit / Apthorus coniug(i) / optimae castae / et sibi*[69]

The use of the term *medicae* suggests that this woman was working as a general physician and was viewed as having a professional level of skill in this field. Although she may still have specialised in female disorders this term would suggest that she acted as a general practitioner.

Many such inscriptions, however, show that these women, although being referred to as doctors, were still fulfilling their domestic role. This can be seen by documenting their skills as an effective healer among their other domestic abilities. This is seen in the following inscription

*d. m. s. / Iuliae Saturinae / ann. XXXXV / uxori incomparabili / medicae optimae / mulieri sanctissimae, / Cassius Philippus / maritus ob meritis* (sic), */ h. s. e. S. t. t. l.*[70]

It is clear from this that although she is called a *medicae* this was seen as an extension of her domestic role. The use here of the term *medicae* suggests that her actions must have been seen to be at least of the level of other professional healers but whether she was held to a different standard than her male colleagues is unclear.

---

[69] CIL VI 7581 'To the sacred spirits of my Primilla, physician, daughter of L. Vibius Melito, she lived 44 years, 30 of them with L. Cocceius Apthorus without complaint. Apthorus made this for his excellent and chaste wife and for himself.'

[70] CIL II 497 'Sacred to the divine spirits of Iulia Saturnina, 45 years old, incomparable wife, excellent physician, most pious woman. Cassius Phillipus, her husband, made this because of her merits. She is laid here. May the earth be light on you.'

There are also literary references to women who have been praised by their communities for their abilities in healing. Antiochis of Tlos was even honoured with a statue.[71] This shows that in her case she was making meaningful contributions beyond the domestic environment and we could assume beyond merely the female population. It also shows that although much of the expert healing carried out by women would have been mostly to benefit other women it is obvious that many of them took this further and treated a broader section of society.

Although there is variation in the status of medical physicians of both genders, this did not seem to be highly influenced by the gender of the physician. Instead it seems to be decided by their class.[72] This could suggest that there is little difference between a male or female physician. This does not seem likely, however, as the written sources suggest and encourage a distinction between genders.

Another professional aspect of healing in which women were involved was wet nursing. In contrast to other medical positions this appeared to represent a more permanent position and seemed to be an informal member of the family.[73] This can be seen by the giving of gifts from successful nurslings to their nurses. Although among the aristocracy it was more common for them to hire an individual wet nurse for a long period, there were also public wet nurses who would provide care for the public in the forums and could be hired when necessary. The significance of wet nurses was much greater in the Roman world than in our society primarily on account of the higher mortality rate amongst both infants and nursing mothers.

In contrast many writers such as Tacitus and Quintilian urge mothers to breast feed their own children if able as a means of increasing affection between them and to prevent the wet nurse from having influence over the child.[74] There was a general view that with milk there was also a transfer of morals and so it was seen as best that a moral woman should breastfeed herself to pass on her morality.[75] This occupation is one in which a woman holds great sway over the development of a

---

[71] Lucian, *Alexander,* 6, 15-17; 19, 29.
[72] Bailey (2012:70); Nutton (2004:196-197).
[73] Joshel (1986:5).
[74] Tacitus, *Dialogus de oratoribus,* 28 - 29; Quintilian, *Institutio Oratoria,* 1. 4. 4 - 11.
[75] Soranus, *Gynecology,* 2. 87.; Favorinus (from Aulus Gellius, ) 12. 1. 8, 11-15, 20.

child. This was especially true since women continued to breast feed their children to an older age than we do in the modern world.

## 5 – Conclusions

It is clear that we can position healing within the domestic role. Although healing may have been an official duty of the *paterfamilias* they did not usually have direct involvement in performing healing tasks. This was seen to be a result of differing gender roles in Roman society which often separated the *paterfamilias* from close contact with those in his care. This separation is seen to be even greater in the case of the rural *domus* in which we see a more formal transfer of the healing responsibility to a woman or other representative.

Substantial variations can also be identified in Roman medicine between urban and rural areas. The populations in rural areas were more persistent in their use of magic and religious approaches to healing. They also tended towards domestic treatment without calling on a professional physician. This can be related to their increased familiarity with local pharmaceuticals which reduced the need for the imported treatments which were applied by professionals.

There were varying opinions expressed about whether treatments themselves were the most significant aspect of healing. This may be attributed to the differing views of the literate and illiterate people although the latter are poorly represented through our dependence on written sources. The modern view that Roman medicine focused entirely on the pharmaceuticals has been propagated through an overdependence on Pliny who promoted this opinion.

The need for a family member to remain appraised of good local physicians was also explained in its context as a product of the Roman medical system. The relationship between Greek and Roman medicine was also considered with the Greek influence on the underlying concepts of Italian medicine identified. The extent of training for both male and female physicians was discussed which illustrated that neither can be regarded as overly formal and a lack of training was not something which hindered female physicians.

This chapter has also established that, although remedies may be promoted as the core aspect of Roman medicine, the role of the healer was also significant. This was particularly true in respect to the lower classes and those in rural environments. Through modern interpretations it was shown that the healer was a major component of Roman medicine, both in an abstract sense but also as a practical part of the healing process.

We have also seen that women were active participants in professional Roman medicine. They fulfilled roles associated with their specific genders, as midwives, gynaecologists and wet-nurses, as well as providing aid to the general public; some to the extent that they received public honours.

# III - Medicine, Women and Society

## 1 – Introduction

Having established that medicine can be seen as part of the domestic role I will now explore what the female duties in healing can tell us about their role in Roman society. This will shed light not only on the women in domestic healing but also on female professionals. To achieve this I will make reference to ancient texts, particularly Soranus and Pliny, to chart the involvement of women in healing and identify trends in their roles and rights. The evidence for this chapter is drawn from Appendix 1 which summarises the treatments found in Soranus, Pliny and Dioscorides. This is especially significant for sections 4 and 5 which explain and explore the trends in this data.

## 2 – Changes in Female Healers Through Time

To begin we must consider the nature of the female healer as represented in Soranus. While his introduction makes clear that midwives would often be female, he rarely defines with certainty what gender was to apply a given treatment within his work.[76] Indeed, although thoroughly outlining how a treatment was to be applied he rarely specifies the qualifications of the practitioner. On occasion however he does specify who is to carry out an action. In these situations he most commonly identifies the midwife as the practitioner. An example can be found in book 3 section 32. Here, although a midwife is identified as a practitioner, the illness does not directly relate to parturition, instead being a complication possibly long after the event.[77] So in this situation we infer that Soranus identifies the practitioner since it may be unclear that this treatment falls within their duties. As a result we could infer that in those cases where no practitioner is identified it is either clear who was to perform the treatment or that the identity of the treater was insignificant.

The latter interpretation is supported as, although anointing and bathing are the most common forms of treatment in Soranus, only once does he suggest that you may need the assistance of a

---

[76] Soranus, *Gynecology*, 1.4.
[77] Soranus, *Gynecology*, 3.32.

professional anointer.[78] In all other circumstances anyone could seemingly apply the treatment. This parallels with the findings of Chapter Two which showed that the Romans focussed on the treatments rather than the practitioner. While Soranus does casually refer to the presence of a doctor in the event of a difficult birth, throughout the rest of the text we must infer that the instructions are mostly directed at the midwife and thus were to be carried out by women.[79] Soranus unfortunately remains mute on whether this physician was already meant to be present at the birth or whether they were summoned after it was clear that there were problems. The earlier section discussing the birth, however, makes no mention of the presence of a doctor, only of three midwives or other women to assist with the birth; and so we must theorise that the physician was sent for out of necessity rather than being a part of the normal birth process.[80]

So it is clear that many of the treatments in Soranus were performed by women with the involvement of men being reserved only for dangerous situations. Although this relates to the content of his work, when we find examples of similar treatments in earlier texts where men are the practitioners, we can observe a change.

On account of Pliny's focus on the substances used for the treatments rather than the methods of treatment, few references make clear who is to perform a treatment. As Pliny aimed to preserve an older and more traditional form of Roman medicine we can assume that many of these treatments were to have been carried out within the home. As it has been established that women in the domestic space may often carry out healing, they may well have applied many of the treatments outlined in Pliny. There is, however, no way of establishing this from the text so it provides little evidence.

In the remedies of Pliny which pertain to women we find that most were to be applied by the woman herself or by other women such as midwives.[81] This parallels Soranus' representation of the presence of female healers, at least in relation to 'women's diseases'. In contrast Pliny provides at

---

[78] See p. 8 n. 15; Soranus, *Gynecology*, 3. 15.
[79] Soranus, *Gynecology*, 4.7.
[80] Soranus, *Gynecology*, 2.5.
[81] Pliny, *Naturalis Historiae*, 20.3, 20.18, 20.34.

least one account in which the involvement of the female patient is strictly discouraged: *putant conceptus adiuvari adalligato semine, si terram non adtigerit, partus vero, si in arietis lana alligatum inscientis lumbis fuerit, ita ut protinus ab enixu rapiatur extra domum.*[82]

This section shows that the female patient must be unaware that this treatment is being carried out. So here a woman is not only unable to perform the treatment: she is also prevented from being aware of it.

The presentation of women as the primary healers in cases of 'women's diseases' is also found in Dioscorides, where it is most often the patient herself who carries out the treatment.[83] This, however, can only be established based on the types of treatments used. Again we find no direct statement that the healer was a specialist or any reference to their gender.

From the presentations in these three works we can see that it is only in the work of Soranus where the participation of a female physician is specified. Although fairly evident that the works of Pliny and Dioscorides refer to female physicians, these texts do not provide anything more specific than inferred participation. This illustrates a change in the status of female physicians within this period.

A similar change can also be seen in the way female patients are viewed. While Pliny clearly indicates that he felt it unnecessary to give women control of their bodies, claiming instead that female health and treatment should be managed by providing or performing treatments without their knowledge, this view of medical practice is not evident by the time of Soranus. He, indeed, suggests that placebos may be used to aid in a woman's treatment at her request, although he believes that these objects have no medical benefit.[84] This difference may also be explained on account of Soranus' scepticism, which would undoubtedly clash with a treatment that somehow required the patient's

---

[82] Pliny, *Naturalis Historiae*, 20. 3 "It is generally thought that the seed of this plant will facilitate conception if a woman carries it attached to her person, before it has touched the ground; and that it has the effect of aiding parturition, if it is first wrapped in ram's wool, and then tied round the woman's loins, without her knowing it, care being taken to carry it out of the house the instant she is delivered."
[83] Dioscorides, *De Materia Medica,* 1.1.2, 1.2.2, 1.4.2, 1.7.4.
[84] Soranus, *Gynecology,* 3. 43.

ignorance of the procedure; but this would not change that it was at the request of a woman not the *paterfamilias*.[85]

The period of the early Empire represented a general rise in the status of women. In early Rome we find women being confined to the home or veiled as in the Greek world.[86] In contrast we find presentations of the women of the Julio-Claudian family taking ever increasing positions of status.[87] This increasing power was apparently not only confined to the ruling class but to a broad group of society.[88] With the increased rights to interact with the public world and the associated capacity for gaining prestige it is unsurprising that we find a similar increase in female healers.

In the work of Soranus we see the activity of numerous professionals and laymen in administering different treatments. As outlined above the vast majority of treatments in Soranus do not specify who was to provide them and so could likely be applied by anyone. We do, though, find treatments that are to be carried out by midwives, anointers, wet nurses and doctors in various situations. This shows a greater concern for the wellbeing of the patient than in Pliny or Dioscorides where no such references can be found. So again this illustrates an increasing concern for female patients. The clear use of midwives and wet nurses also shows the growing realm of professional female healers. This is emphasised as Soranus differentiates between a professional and experienced midwife and other female attendants at the birth.[89] A sizable amount of the *Gynaecology* is concerned with identifying the appropriate qualities of both midwives and wet nurses. This work also outlines the responsibility of these positions; many of these duties afford great authority to the practitioner. A midwife, for example, is responsible for determining if a child it to be weaned, or to advise exposure.[90] A wet nurse would also be responsible for the primary medical treatment of a baby, most often through her milk but also as the main carer.[91]

---

[85] Temkin (1956:xxxi).
[86] Maximus, *Factorum ac dictorum memorabilium,* Llibri IX 6.3.10.
[87] Tacitus, *Annales,* 12.1-9; Suetonius, *Nero,* 28.
[88] MacMullen (1980:210).
[89] Soranus, *Gynecology,* 2.4-5.
[90] Soranus, *Gynecology,* 2. 6.
[91] Soranus, *Gynecology,* 2.87, 2.118.

Although it is clear that these occupations existed in the time of Pliny the Elder and Dioscorides, these writers avoid reference to them. Even in this period, however, there are numerous references to gifts being given particularly to wet nurses.[92] These gifts were often substantial. Pliny the Younger notably gifted his wet nurse a farm and the staff to manage it.[93] It also appears common for wet nurses to be manumitted during or after their service.[94] The manner in which these instances are framed is suggestive: namely, although these women were seen as significant and so rewarded, it was still seen as taboo to mention them – at least in the time of Pliny the Elder. Here, of course, Pliny may be promoting an antiquarian perspective and so be discouraging the use of nurses, viewing their activity as a form of decadence. Importantly, this perspective cannot be attributed to Dioscorides.

## 3 – The Status of Female Physicians

The terms *medicae* (general doctors) and *obstetrices* (midwives), although likely different, are difficult to separate based on the available evidence and so are usually best discussed as a single field.[95] As has been discussed in Chapter Two, these women could clearly be quite respected in a community and were acting for the benefit of the community at large rather than for their own homes. While they may have always been in the minority, it seems likely that female physicians would have been well accepted in Rome.

If we follow the traditional view that the professional physician (as a category of person providing a service) was imported from Greece and that with them came Greek medical views, then Roman women would likely have been accepted in medicine as they had in Greece.[96] This cultural process was however slow and so there may well have been initial resistance. This resistance however seems to have been felt across physicians of both genders.[97]

---

[92] Bradley (1986:204).
[93] Pliny the Younger, *Epistulae*, 6.3.
[94] Joshel (1986:16); Bradley (1986:204 - 206).
[95] Jackson (1988:191 n. 12); Nickel (1979:115 - 118); King (1986:55; 59-60).
[96] Cushing (1998:44); Hyginus, *Fabula*, 274. 10-13.
[97] Hillman (2004:22).

The acceptance of female physicians is to be expected since they were traditionally used in medicine. Certainly the domestic and folk healing which would have been more prevalent in early Italic communities would depend substantially on the women to have provided supportive care and likely to be familiar with drug lore. Additionally, for support in birthing we continue to see the use of a female community to aid in the process which is a clear reflection of such systems in earlier periods.[98]

The *medicae* are known from Soranus to have treated practically all women's diseases. Issues arising in relation to menstruation and parturition may be the conditions we most quickly think of, but there was a broad array of possible ailments, many of which were seen as quite dangerous. Parturition was mostly the responsibility of a midwife whereas a woman suffering full retention of the menstrual flux, which Soranus identifies as dangerous, would likely have been attended by a *medicae*.[99] Particularly if this illness becomes chronic, complex treatments may be required such as the *metasyncratic* cure as well as applications of moderately dangerous substances such as hellebore.[100]

Soranus also provides an insight into the status of an *obstetrix* when he lists their duties during and after a birth, particularly that they choose whether or not a child is worth rearing.[101] He provides a detailed account of the characteristics to be considered. While Soranus does not specify, we should assume that the decision itself still rested with the *paterfamilias* as to whether a child was to be raised or exposed and that the *obstetrix* merely provided advice. But even this was a substantial right and illustrated that they must have been regarded as experts.

As with male doctors, the status and thus pay of female physicians would have related to their class.[102] Based on inscriptions and other references we find that most women claiming to be *medicae* are related to a *medicus*, usually either their father or husband.[103] Thus we can assume that they were

---

[98] Soranus, *Gynecology*, 2.4-5.
[99] Soranus, *Gynecology*, 3.9.
[100] Soranus, *Gynecology*, 3.15-16; the metasyncretic cure focused on destabilising or irritating a patient's body. In the case of Soranus this involved fasting separated by specific diets of bread, pungent foods, vegetable brain or fish, fowl and pork. Then repeat while inducing vomiting during the fasts. C.f. Weckowicz and Liebel-Weckowicz (1990:30); Everett (2012:49).
[101] Soranus, *Gynecology*, 2.10.
[102] Scarborough (1969:110-112).
[103] Flemming (2007:260); Bailey (2012:71).

likely drawn from the same classes. Male physicians were usually of low status, most commonly being freedmen or having freedmen as ancestors.[104] This was particularly true for the doctors who treated the mainstream of Roman society. In contrast those from the upper echelons preferred to recruit physicians from a likewise higher status.[105] It is these physicians who are paid at extraordinary rates and tend to gain more fame.

The complex remedies contained in Soranus strongly suggest that any female physician who was to perform them would have required some familiarity with medical theory.[106] Without this grounding the remedies would not make any sense and, even if she felt confident to simply apply them as Soranus instructs, it is unlikely that the patient would have been eager to proceed without some explanation. Having this understanding of medical theory it seems likely that such a physician would be able to administer treatments for a complete spectrum of diseases. Soranus himself argues that women's diseases do not really exist as they only differ in their manifestation, but that their underlying forms were the same as all other diseases.[107] So while it cannot be shown with absolute certainty that female healers also treated male diseases it seems almost certain that they would be capable. Additionally this shows that their duties may well have included the treating of women for any disease rather than just those seen as particular to their gender.

The traditional foundation mythology of female healers suggests that ancient women were refusing treatment from male practitioners to the detriment of their health.[108] The myth of Agnodike suggests that the principle cause for her engaging in medical practice was the high mortality resulting from women refusing treatment from male physicians. Additionally we find that she was so popular as a female physician that it resulted in the law prohibiting female practice being changed. [109]As a piece of mythology, this can provide insight into the way in which ancient societies function.[110] Whether or not these myths were based on true events, the creators of the myth found it reasonable that such things

---

[104] Scarborough (1969:110-112).
[105] Scarborough (1969:111).
[106] Soranus, *Gynecology*, 3.15-16.
[107] Soranus, *Gynecology*, 3.5.
[108] King (1986:53-54).
[109] Hyginus, *Fabula*, 274. 10-13.
[110] Powell (2009:12-14, 647-649); Brillante (1990:105-108).

may occur. Although these are set in a Greek context it seems unlikely that they would be distinct in this respect. So we can establish that, although not necessarily based on their degree of expertise, female healers were preferred by female patients. This is also indicated by Soranus who clearly expects that most midwives and gynaecologists would be female – although it should be remembered that he himself is an example of a male in such a position.[111]

The suggestion that a suitable practitioner should be literate and familiar with the relevant literature may either be taken to illustrate that women were often literate, or it may have implied that most women were unsuitable to the task.[112] There would have been no doubt about Soranus's meaning to a contemporary reader; however, without knowing the rates of female, or indeed male, literacy, we cannot tell. With most education in basic literature occurring in the' primary' stage of Roman education it seems likely that this would be all that was required to understand the text of Soranus and thus other gynaecological writings. Although Soranus was written in Greek rather than Latin it is probable that literacy education taught both languages simultaneously and so we could still expect students to reach reasonable competence early in their education. The language used in Soranus is confusing only in regards to its vocabulary and is otherwise in reasonably clear prose. The 'high school' level education would likely have had little effect on the capacity for a student to understand prose as it focused on poetry and philosophy. Additionally, this vocabulary would likely have been known by any professional midwife or gynaecologist as a necessary vocabulary for their occupation, so by using primary grade literacy skills it is likely they could understand these gynaecological texts.

We are also unable to tell whether men would have preferred their wives and daughters to be attended by male or female physicians. The republican sources paint a negative view of female healers, though this is no greater than that of male Greek doctors. Pliny, at least, would likely see female healers as a threat to the purity of Roman traditions and the status of the *paterfamilias*. Soranus in his strict conditions on the suitability of healers does seem to encourage the view that a

---

[111] Soranus, *Gynecology,* 1.3-4, 3.3.
[112] Soranus, *Gynecology,* 1.3.

male may have been more suitable.[113] It also seems clear that Soranus expects that many of his readers would be female and this possibly explains why he is not more overt in his recommendation of male physicians. The mere survival of female healers indicates that their services must have been required. As Roman women would often have been under the *potestas* of a father, the *manus* of a husband or the supervision of a tutor, we could also infer that these men did not prevent the use of a female healer.[114] If a woman was under the supervision of a tutor this control may be minimal especially if she was married in *manu*.[115] For elite women we find notable examples of independence and, while women may theoretically be subject to another's *potestas*, this may not have been applicable.[116]

## 4 – Trends in Medical Treatment

Using the references collected we can begin to see trends in the types of treatments that were applied by men and women.

In Pliny we find that 680 out of 1226 treatments were administered orally, either as food or drink, thus forming the vast majority of the treatments he lists.[117] A comparable 92 of 189 treatments in Dioscorides are also of this type.[118] In Soranus, however, we find only 67 of 434 references are of this type. In contrast, we find many more treatments dependant on bathing or anointing, with 73 references;[119] while in Pliny, we find only 46 examples and of those listed none pertain to women's diseases.[120] In Dioscorides we find 16 examples of bathing treatments 12 of which relate to female

---

[113] Soranus, *Gynecology*, 1.3-4.
[114] Gardner (1986:5).
[115] Schulz (1951:185-186); Gardner (1986:15-16); Matthews (1995:767). See too the fear that excessive accrual of wealth by women would ultimately effect manpower and the functions of Empire, Hopwood (2004:141 - 147).
[116] See chapter II. 2.
[117] 'oral decoction', 'oral (mastication)', 'oral drink and injection', masticant, confection, drink, 'oral drink topical', draught, 'gargle or drink', masticant, pill, 'drink and liniment', 'drink, topical', 'drink or topical', 'masticant, topical', 'masticant and topical', 'drink or smell', 'oral, drink', 'drink topical', 'oral, injection', 'oral topical'.
[118] Drink, 'drink or topical', 'drink, purge', lozenge, masticant, oral.
[119] Anointment, bath, 'bath, other', 'bath, oral', fomentation, massage, 'bath, rubeficiant', rubificant.
[120] Bath, injection or fomentation, topical ointment, ointment.

ailments.[121] The majority of the remaining remedies in Soranus (142 treatments) are topical.[122] Similarly we find 332 examples of topical remedies in Pliny;[123] while in Dioscorides we find 45 examples. [124]

As Pliny and Dioscorides present the more general form of medicine, in contrast to the specialist work of Soranus which focuses on female conditions, we can assume that most ancient Roman medicine was principally based on remedies delivered orally. Soranus, though, uses such treatments sparingly, forming only 15% of his cures. As Soranus is the only work where we can establish with certainty that these treatments were performed by women, we can surmise that the primary remedies females applied were based on bathing, anointing and topical treatments. This contrasts with the trend for oral treatments to be applied by male physicians.

Based on Soranus alone, it is difficult to establish whether women were restricted to these forms of treatment through social constraints, or if they were perceived to be the form of treatment most beneficial to alleviating or ameliorating the symptoms associated with 'women's diseases'. If we compare the treatments found in Soranus with similar treatments in Pliny, we find that the former makes greater use of oral remedies for these diseases. Of Pliny's remedies, however, there is still an above average use of other forms of treatment, especially bathing. This would seem to indicate that the form of treatment depended on those who administered it rather than the gender of the patient. This theory is also supported by Dioscorides who provides numerous references to orally administered treatments. One should note, however, that the treatments delivered orally are almost exclusively for bringing on or aiding menstruation. Additionally we do find an above average number of bathing treatments in relation to other forms of female illness. It seems quite likely that the

---

[121] 'vap, Bath', 'sitz bath' 'sitz baths', 'sitz bath of fumigation', 'topical, bath', 'v.sup. and sitz bath'
[122] Cataplasm, cerates, compress, 'other, topical', plaster, pledget, poultice, 'poultice, plaster', 'poultice, diet', salve, 'sup, poultice', topical, 'topical, compress', 'topical, other'.
[123] Depilatory, drink or topical, drink topical, 'drink,topical', ear drops, eye drops, folk topical, 'fomentation, topical', masticant and topical, 'masticant, topical', ointment, 'oral, drink, topical', 'oral, topical', plaster, poultice, topical, 'topical bandage', 'topical, emetic', 'topical ointment', 'topical, gargle', topical/folk
[124] Cataplasm, depilatory, drink or topica, ointment, plaster, poultice, salve, 'sub or poultices' topical, 'topical (liniment)', 'topical, bath'; The remaining unexplained data are mostly either general references to the properties of the pharmaceuticals especially in Dioscorides, as well as folk practices as found in Pliny. The large number of un-included references in Soranus are mostly folk medicines, suppositories and surgery or bleedings these making up at least 107 of the 152 examples not used in the above statistics.

absence of or difficulty in menstruating represented occasions where a professional physician may have been required and thus this may explain the presence of oral treatments.

Additionally we should consider whether these treatments formed a significant part of the entirety of the Roman medical system. All evidence seems to suggest that these 'women's diseases' were significant. References to such diseases and treatments are found in all of our accounts. There are 26 references to such diseases in Dioscorides and a similar percentage in Pliny. From this, although we cannot establish how much of practiced medicine was of this form, we can show that approximately a quarter of Roman diseases were restricted to women.

From these general trends I will now consider more specific treatments used by women and the possible significance of these. Particularly, I will consider pharmaceuticals which the Romans considered dangerous.

We find only one reference to opium in Soranus.[125] This account associates the opium with a concoction comprising vinegar, hypocist and acacia juice.[126] Notably this treatment was not intended for oral delivery but was instead a vaginal injection. However, based on the warnings in Pliny, we should still expect that the use was moderately dangerous. This concoction was intended to stop a uteral haemorrhage, a condition that Soranus believed was dangerous.[127] Again this is a situation where it would be useful to have clarification of who was to perform the treatment. Soranus outlines other means of preventing bleeding, including hooks, ligatures and stiches. These procedures may well have been more associated with *medici*. However, even if this is the case, we cannot tell whether this physician would be male or female. The use of cupping which follows supports the interpretation that this would be treated by a *medicus* as cupping vessels were often used in art as a symbol of physicians.[128]

---

[125] The poppy was considered lethal by Pliny, *Naturalis Historiae*, 20.76.
[126] Soranus, *Gynecology*, 3. 41; Hypocist is the solidified juice of *Cytinus hypocistis* used as a tonic and astringent; Little, et al., (Hypocist)The Shorter Oxford English Dictionary(1973:1009).
[127] Soranus, *Gynecology*, 3. 40.
[128] Soranus, *Gynecology*, 3. 41; Scarborough (1969:pl. 47).

Pliny advises of the dangers of poppy use, especially in the form of opium. However, he does list a variety of treatments for which he endorses the use of the poppy.[129] None of the ailments he references related to female illnesses and so it seems that opium was used sparingly on women, possibly on account of its risks. This is an interesting trend. The lack of references provides no evidence that female physicians were to apply opium, which may represent a restriction of their medical role. As most of the treatments presented in Pliny were applicable to either gender this does not mean that women could not use opium, however its use as an analgesic, especially in war, would not apply to women. Its use in such circumstances was likely as a last resort on patients with a limited chance of survival. There are numerous reasons why opium may not be used for women's complaints or on them for pain relief. Firstly the higher pain tolerance of women may make such use less necessary. Secondly it may reflect a concern that women could not handle the strength of the substance, although this seems unlikely as it has been established that opium was still applied to them. Finally if, as suggested earlier, female physicians were restricted from applying opium this may have made the use of opium for women's diseases unfeasible through a lack of suitable physicians.

These trends are important as the preference for topical treatments grants less power to these female physicians than oral remedies. Oral consumption represents a breach of our bodily barrier.[130] When we consider medicines in our own society we can see a clear hierarchy in the perceived power of treatments:[131]

Surgery > Injection > Ingestion > Topical Application

Inspection of this hierarchy reveals that it correlates with the degree to which the body is penetrated with surgery being the most extreme and topical applications involving no penetration. This concern for the bodily boundary is also clear when we consider other events which involve the breach of this

---

[129] Pliny, *Naturalis Historiae*, 20.76-80.
[130] Meigs (1997:96); Douglas (1997:36).
[131] In this hierarchy '>' is utilised to illustrate the term on left is more significant than that on the right.

boundary; sex, toileting and eating being the most notable.[132] All of these events are heavily associated with rituals.

Food can thus be seen as a means of incorporating both the symbolic and physical aspects of a material.[133] Topical treatments do not entail the same dangers nor the same benefits, and so the application of a dangerous substance externally represents less danger and ascribes less power or status to the physician. Although it gives slightly greater authority and status other means of internalising a treatment such as the suppositories which are so common in Soranus are still not as significant as ingestion. The exception to this is surgery that, as now, is ascribed a greater significance on account of its danger and immediate effects.

## 5 - What Female Physicians Did Not Do

We now turn to consideration of what practices or treatments female physicians would not have performed.

A major field of medicine in which women were unrepresented was surgery.[134] This absence can be easily understood if we consider the scope of surgery and the means of training. The training of physicians was carried out by apprenticeship and so surgeons too must have learnt their art through experience.[135] As the majority of surgery that was performed was carried out in response to battle wounds this left little opportunity for women to gain experience in the art and ensured that this speciality was restricted to men.[136] This inability to train was exemplified as dissection was not permitted in the Roman world,[137] thus preventing exposure to and understanding of the workings of the body and so make successful surgery unachievable.

---

[132] Fieldhouse (1986:173); Griffin (1981:24-25).
[133] Fiddes (1991:279-280); Meigs (1997); Fischler (1988).
[134] Surgery here excludes normal childbirth particularly as this doesn't entail the cutting of a patient.
[135] Flemming (2007:260-261); cf.Adcock (1945:9).
[136] Hippocrates, *de Medico,* 9.219; Drabkin (1944:336-337).
[137] With the exception of Alexandria where dissection and supposedly vivisection were permitted since it is required for mummification. See Edelstein (1935).

There may have been ethical reasons which could explain the female absence from surgery. Most notably, a key quality of a surgeon was to ignore the pain of the patient, as surgery was performed without anaesthetic.[138] This quality I expect would have been seen as uncommon and unbecoming of a woman where as such a trait was preferred in the case of men.

Additionally, the application of dangerous oral remedies which is absent from the treatments performed by women can be understood in terms of the gender roles and the relationship between men and women. As women were traditionally seen to be subject to the control of a male guardian and this was viewed as their natural position in society,[139] if a woman were to apply a dangerous treatment, especially to a male patient, this would place the woman temporarily in a position of greater authority than the male patient. Although possible, and in some circumstances likely, that this occurred it would have been something to have been avoided as it broke with social mores and traditions. In contrast it is clear that a wet nurse may hold authority over a male infant, though this was probably acceptable as the wet nurse herself was likely under the control of the *paterfamilias* and there is no way in which the infant could hold authority over the woman.

## 6 - Conclusions

Through an examination of the treatments women could apply we can see that these were highly socially regulated and reflected the preference to maintain the status of men and so not subject them to the views of a woman. These treatments illustrate that female specialists must have had an understanding of medical theory which would likely have allowed them to treat a wide array of conditions.

The ancient evidence illustrates a change in the presentation of women both as the healer and patient between the times of Pliny and Soranus. Where Pliny accepts that there are diseases particular to women this view was refuted in Soranus' work. Similarly Pliny and Dioscorides make no mention of female healers while Soranus acknowledges them regularly despite preferring male

---

[138] Bliquez (1981:12).
[139] See chapter III.3.

practitioners. As a patient Soranus also gives greater rights to the patient than the earlier works. This is seen to parallel with increasing female autonomy in society more broadly.

Female physicians were likely well acknowledged by the end of the period under consideration and were given notable responsibilities, especially in advising on the survival of the child. They were seemingly drawn from a similar social status as their male counterparts who were usually of a notably low position. Based on the historical context we can also show that female healers were likely preferred by female patients and not shunned by their male guardians.

While it is clear that women occasionally did perform treatments with dangerous substances, these were usually applied in a manner to offset their danger compared to the way male physicians would likely apply them. Surgery, as a form of dangerous treatment, is seen to exclude women, mostly out of an inability to train them. It has also been possible to discern an aversion to such an occupation being filled by women on account of gender roles.

# IV - Understanding Healing

## 1 – Introduction

The purpose of this chapter is to utilise the evidence of the treatments females could apply (in contrast to their male counterparts) as a means of understanding the risks, and thus power, of specific pharmaceuticals as they were viewed in Roman culture. The tendency for women to apply treatments topically, as seen in the previous chapter, allows for a new strategy by which to consider the power of pharmaceuticals which appears regularly in part 6 of this chapter. A variety of other approaches have been used to reconstruct the significance of different pharmaceuticals; however, it is clear from section 6 that this investigation has greatly benefitted from an understanding of gender roles. The assessment of particular pharmaceuticals is of course only a select sample, as, in order to perform this analysis for even the majority of medicines would far exceed the length of this thesis. Instead, this section aims to provide a framework for future enquiries of this type and to establish the viability of such investigations.

## 2 - Background of methods

This chapter will begin by outlining the approaches taken and the forms of evidence to be used to expose what can be learnt about pharmacy and pharmaceuticals in Roman society based on these approaches.

In studies which examine the effectiveness of Roman medicine it is clear that the treatments were mostly ineffective. The 'perceived' effect of these substances can be explained using the meaning effect. So, if it were generally believed that a treatment was effective, then there was an increased chance of healing occurring and that positive results would be more memorable.[140] This effect is also tied to quality of the treatments which are applied. For instance, if a test group is given aspirin, those who take pills of a known brand will experience stronger results than those who are given generic

---

[140] Moerman and Jonas (2002:471) On the 'Barnum' effect and the tendency to accept positive information and ignore negative suggestions, see Dutton (1988:326).

medicines.[141] More substantially patients may automatically ascribe meaning and power to remedies based on cultural ideas. In a test in which medical students were given either one or two red or blue pills, all placebos, and are informed they are participating in a test of stimulants and depressants those who were given red pills reported symptoms of taking a stimulant while those with blue pills report symptoms of depressants.[142] Those who were given multiple pills also exhibited a greater response than those with one.

We can also gain a greater understanding of Roman medicines based on the informal controls applied to their use as a means of regulating them. Such practices are found in all traditional forms of drug use in the modern world so it can be inferred that this is a universal human characteristic.[143] Modern examples can be seen in phrases such as 'don't drink and drive' or 'don't drink before noon'.[144] These are more than merely sayings but are beliefs which should not be broken, people need not consider such a saying to not drink in the morning; it would simply feel wrong both to the individual and those around them to break them.[145] In the case of less dangerous substances these social controls are often easily broken or stretched. As the substances become more dangerous, such as with heroin use in the modern world, these restrictions become more rigid with less freedom to modify or break from them.[146]

These social controls generally allow for much safer drug use and are among the reasons that drugs are most dangerous when first created. While there were substantial problems with alcohol abuse during and immediately after the prohibition in the United States, alcohol quickly became a drug which could be used with relatively little danger.[147] This is a result of increased familiarity with the substance and the associated introduction of social controls.

---

[141] Branthwaite and Cooper (1981).
[142] Blackwell, et al. (1972); Cattaneo, et al. (1970); Schapira, et al. (1970).
[143] Weil (1998:99); Keenan (2004:71-72).
[144] Du Toit (1997:114).
[145] Moore (1993:60); Zinberg (1984:9-10).
[146] See the regulation of 'trips' in Moore (1993:61).
[147] Zinberg (1984:9).

Similar controls can be seen in food consumption when the embodying of a substance is seen as negative. An example can be found in the 18th century when young women were known to have starved themselves, especially avoiding meat, as an appetite for food was associated with a desire for sexual pleasure.[148] This is astoundingly similar to social regulations of drug use, as again we find a social trend designed to protect these females from the risks of meat consumption. From the described social controls, we see that substances that are more controlled are seen as more dangerous, and those which are more dangerous are, based on the meaning effect, more powerful. Using these contemporary methodologies will allow a reconstruction of the perceived power of Roman pharmaceuticals.

The work of Zinberg has identified a correlation between drug, set and setting.[149] While he applies this insight to an understanding of addiction it is clear from his study that these three features are highly relevant to drug use in general.[150] I will develop an understanding of Roman medicine through discussion of the set and setting of healing. The following sentences shall explain how I will apply these terms to my study. The 'drug' component of this enquiry is merely the substance being used and its associated physical effects. The setting is the physical environment in which a treatment took place, whether this is the home of the patient or a formalised place of treatment such as a forum. The set is the most difficult to interpret as this is the social environment in which treatment takes place; however, this relates closely to the involvement of women in healing and should be reinterpreted in light of their involvement.

A close investigation of the types of language used in relation to medicine will provide a greater insight into how the Roman people understood healing. This method is effective firstly because language shapes and reflects the thoughts of the culture and secondly because it may give insights into the metaphorical construction of ideas.[151] The work of George Lakoff and Mark Johnson explores

---

[148] Brumberg (1997:168-174).
[149] These were defined by Zinberg (1984:5) "drug (the pharmacologic action of the substance itself), set (the attitude of the person at the time of use, including his personality structure), and setting (the influence of the physical and social setting within which the use occurs)."
[150] Zinberg (1984:5).
[151] Clark (1998:163-169).

this approach and shows that our existence is shaped by metaphors which are not perceived but nonetheless influence the way in which we conceive of complex issues such as an argument.[152]

## 3 - The 'Setting' of Medicine

Medical treatment could occur in a variety of situations and this can provide information on the influence of treatment. Indeed a variation in environment may be one way of differentiating between professional and amateur medicine.

Medical treatment in this period could occur in three possible environments. Firstly, it could occur in the house of the patient with the physician being summoned. This was the most traditional form of treatment and reflected the form of medicine practised in Roman Italy, which emphasised domestic healing.[153] Secondly, it could occur in a shop-like venue assigned specifically for medical treatment. These were often mobile venues and so would also have been common in smaller communities which may not have possessed a standing population of doctors.[154] Finally, treatment could be performed in the house of the physician.

From Soranus we can see that when a woman was giving birth the physician usually came to the home of the patient.[155] This seemingly applied to all treatments in preparation for the birth, even though these could have been applied in a separate locality.[156] This practice is likely related to the status of women and their traditional association with the domestic space, in that if women were traditionally meant to reside within the house then the treatments of women would more likely take place in this area. This was mostly applicable to the wealthy upper class women of Rome, since those with less wealth may have had to work as a means of earning income which would thus have entailed an existence beyond the home. Additionally it was mainly the women of these upper classes who were likely to call on the assistance of a physician. The ideal which is presented in the literature,

---

[152] An argument is seen to have certain metaphoric parallels which in our culture relate to war whereas if these parallels were to relate to a dance completly different aspects of an argument may be significant and valued, such as harmony rather than winning or losing. Lakoff and Johnson (1980:3-8).
[153] Hillman (2004:22-33).
[154] Jackson (1988).
[155] Soranus, *Gynecology*, 2.67.
[156] Soranus, *Gynecology*, 1.49-56.

however, would still promote that a woman should reside in the home and so it still seems likely that, for birth, the physician would come to the home of the patient regardless of their social status.

In contrast the public wet nurses could usually be found in the forum, an example of the second venue for treatments. This can again be linked to the gender of the patient as the public wet nurses would likely have been used where a mother had died during birth.[157] There are also reports of wet nurses congregating in a forum to seek permanent employment where they would be hired to work at the home of the nurseling. In this form of nursing the mother may well be alive, which could explain the use of domestic healing.

Healing which takes place in the home of the physician was likely to be quite similar in format to treatments which occurred in the forum. This was particularly appropriate if large or specialised equipment was needed, such as basins either for bathing or for the collection of bodily fluids.[158] The use of a space especially designed for performing medical treatments would convey that the environment is a place for healing and so, based on the meaning effect, would increase the likelihood of success and make the treatment seem more powerful and official. It would also have reassured the patient about the proficiency of the physician. The presence of specialised medical equipment would also have given an opportunity for the display of affluence or favour from wealthy patients.[159]

## 4 - The 'Set' of Medical Treatments

As we have seen, there was variation between the types of treatments applied by healers of different genders. Oral treatments were more commonly used by men and so these were likely seen as the more powerful form of treatment.[160] Surgery, to a greater extent than any other, could only be performed by men and so it can be viewed as a dangerous and therefore powerful form of

---

[157] Bradley (1986:207).
[158] Bliquez (1981:11).
[159] Bliquez (1981:12).
[160] See Chapter III. 4.

treatment. This is significant as we find that surgeries were less likely to be performed at the house of the patient and so the setting is also distinct.[161]

We have seen that women may apply medicine both as a professional and as part of her domestic duties. Between these two formats there is great variation in the set of treatment. The use of a professional female healer would suggest a more dangerous illness and the use of more dangerous or complex pharmaceuticals.[162]

It must also be considered how medical treatment was accessed. For example, if a baby was sick who would be able to seek treatment: the midwife, the mother or the father? Would a midwife, as the first point of contact, be allowed to recruit assistance or administer treatments herself? There are indications in the source material that for certain illnesses she would administer a treatment and in most cases she would have to be involved.[163] Further if the *materfamilias* of a household were ill could she seek aid without the intervention of the *paterfamilias*? As was established in chapter two this was likely the ideal; however, through absence of the *paterfamilias*, she must regularly have sought aid by herself.[164] The medical process is quite different if, as is often represented in literature, a mediator is needed between patient and doctor.[165] It seems most probable that a woman could engage a physician without the aid of her husband. This is more probable for those in an urban setting as they would be more likely to have a regular physician. In contrast, in a rural environment it seems less likely that a woman would seek out her own medical aid. As professional healers were less commonly used in these areas and the families themselves more skilled in healing,[166] it is likely that here the woman may treat herself rather than risk employing a doctor of unknown credentials.

As physicians were drawn from many social classes we should also consider the class interactions of the doctor-patient relationship. In our modern culture doctors usually hold the higher status over a

---

[161] Bliquez (1981:11).
[162] For examples of such treatments, see Soranus, *Gynecology*, 1.65, 2.98, 2.118 (App. 1: 0051-0053, 0092, 0104); see chapter III. 2.
[163] Soranus, *Gynecology*, 2.87, 2.118.
[164] Cicero, *Epistulae ad Familiares*, 6.14.4; Cicero, *Epistulae ad Familiares*, 155.14.7.
[165] Plautus, *Menaechmi*, 919-20.
[166] Hillman (2004:21-22); Bailey (2012:82).

patient: the patient follows a doctor to their room and the doctor will usually sit first.[167] In Rome however, not only is the physician likely to be of the same class as the patient, but the relationship appears to be more equal.[168] While the physician does ask questions and give a recommended treatment they are not mandating that this is what must be done and a patient would be free to treat themselves with something else if they felt it more useful.[169] So, while a Roman patient places trust in the recommendations of a physician, they are more involved in their care than we in contemporary times. This shows that the status of Roman physicians should be seen as likely less significant than doctors in modern western medicine.[170]

## 5 – Understanding the Language of Medicine

In relation to the language used relating to medicine we can gain interesting information on how medicine was understood. To begin, Latin differentiates between positive and negative pharmaceuticals with *medicamentum* being used principally of positive treatments and venēnum being used of poisons.[171] This contrasts to Greek where the term φάρμακον can mean either a positive or negative treatment.[172] The variation in Latin suggests that poisons especially were seen as a distinct category which existed beyond accidental medical overdose. It is less correct to claim that *medicamentum* also represented a distinct category as, although less common, this could be applied to a negative pharmaceutical especially with the term *malum*.[173]

Adding to the versatility of *medicamentum*, it may also be used of cosmetics.[174] From this dual role a parallel can be drawn with the idea that Roman medicine, in contrast to the Greek, merely

---

[167] This is particularly noticeable with the absence of a strong class system in Australia.
[168] The contempt expressed in Pliny and the outspoken characters in Plautus suggest that a patient would often aggressively confront a physician. See Plautus, *Menaechmi*, 922.
[169] Without this ability the *herbari* would not have survived as a separate category with this function being taken up by the physicians themselves.
[170] University of Virginia (2007)
[171] Glare, (medicāmentum) Oxford Latin Dictionary (2012: 1197); Glare, (uenēnum) Oxford Latin Dictionary (2012:2234).
[172] Liddell and Scott, Liddell, (φάρμακον)An Intermediate Greek - English Lexicon(2013:855).
[173] Glare, (medicāmentum) Oxford Latin Dictionary (2012: 1197).
[174] Glare, (medicāmentum) Oxford Latin Dictionary (2012: 1197).

attempted to conceal the symptoms of an illness rather than treat its underlying cause.[175] The metaphor that cosmetics are medicine would seem strange to us, specifically because we view medicines as treating a problem while cosmetics merely conceal. From this evidence we find additional insight that Romans considered healing to be related to the apparent symptoms rather than needing enquiry to find something hidden and treat the inferred problem.

If we are to understand properly what is meant by medicine, we must understand what is meant by health. So while *sanitas* may mean health it also conveys a sense of mental wellbeing and "good sense": thus we can say that to have health is also to have good sense.[176] We additionally find that when used in oratory it may mean "freedom form undesirable or debased features".[177] From this we see that the Roman definition of health describes a positive sense of mind and body while we would define health in terms of equilibrium and normality. It is for this reason that we find *sano*, to heal, may also mean to curb a harmful tendency.[178]

## 6 – Establishing the Power of Treatments

It would be impossible in the scope of this work to discuss the relative power of every treatment found in Pliny, Soranus and Dioscorides. So instead I will present selected pharmaceuticals and consider their significance. The pharmaceuticals to be considered are saffron, radish, poppy, *elaterium* (cucumber) and honey

When understanding the use of saffron we find that in 9 out of the 16 examples collected it is applied orally.[179] Of these there are only two examples in Soranus; in neither case is it applied by itself and in only one is it likely the active ingredient.[180] It is also significant that in the treatment where it is an active component it is to be applied by the patient themselves.[181] The absence of the need for any

---

[175] Hillman (2004:78).
[176] Glare, (sanitas) Oxford Latin Dictionary (2012: 1862).
[177] Glare, (sanitas) Oxford Latin Dictionary (2012: 1862).
[178] Glare, (sano) Oxford Latin Dictionary (2012: 1862).
[179] Soranus, *Gynecology*, 2.120; Pliny, *Naturalis Historiae*, 20.79; Dioscorides, *De Materia Medica*, 1.26.2-3 (App. 1: 0116, 1443, 1864, 1865,1866, 1868, 1870, 1873, 1874).
[180] Soranus, *Gynecology*, 2.77. (App. 1: 0069) (active ingredient), Soranus, *Gynecology*, 2.120. (App. 1: 0116).
[181] Soranus, *Gynecology*, 2.77. (App. 1: 0069).

medical practitioner illustrates that this treatment must have been regarded as safe. It is only in the work of Dioscorides where we find treatments of pure saffron.[182] In addition to identifying the general traits of the substance he also provides the lethal dose.[183] The quantity of saffron which he identifies was likely unobtainable, as while 19g may sound small, saffron in the ancient world, as now, was highly labour-intensive to produce and so such an amount would entail a significant cost.[184] His belief that saffron has a lethal dose does suggest that he considers it dangerous. This is supported by the above average tendency for topical application in Dioscorides. In the remedies listed by Pliny, we only encounter saffron in small quantities in other treatments.[185]

The complex treatments which contain saffron suggest a tendency to protect a patient from the power of the pure plant. Similarly when an untrained woman is to administer the substance they only apply it topically; likely another means of reducing risk.[186] This suggests that saffron was regarded as a powerful form of treatment as, though seen as dangerous, it was still used.

Radish is another interesting pharmaceutical to be considered in terms of its status in Roman healing. It is principally applied orally suggesting that is not regarded as overly dangerous or powerful. Among the main uses of Radish is to induce vomiting and so it is unsurprising that we also find an antidote to radish overdose.[187] In Pliny we also find radish used as an amulet, suggesting either substantial medicinal power, in that its proximity results in healing or that it contains magical properties. There are, however, major differences in the use of radishes between Pliny and Soranus: in Soranus we find them used only for the purpose of inducing vomiting,[188] while in Pliny we find that radishes can cure at least 28 illnesses, including a variety of women's complaints that we would expect to find in Soranus.[189]

---

[182] Dioscorides, *De Materia Medica*, 1.26.2-3. (App. 1: 1864,1865, 1868-1872).
[183] General traits Dioscorides, *De Materia Medica*, 1.26.2-3. (App. 1: 1864; 1873).
[184] Deo (2003:1).
[185] Pliny, *Naturalis Historiae*, 20.73, 20.79.(App. 1: 1360, 1443).
[186] Soranus, *Gynecology*, 2.77. (App. 1: 0069).
[187] Pliny, *Naturalis Historiae*, 20.13. (App. 1: 0589).
[188] Soranus, *Gynecology*, 3.15, 3.28, 3.44. (App. 1: 0226, 0295, 0416)
[189] Pliny, *Naturalis Historiae*, 20.13. (App. 1: 0558-0591) see chapter III. 4.

The use of poppy is discussed extensively in Pliny. While he considers all forms of poppy suitable for inducing sleep, the dark poppy, he states, may cause death.[190] His description of poppies contains unique elements: specifically, he lists treatments for which poppy was not to be used.[191] Additionally he includes a section on the testing of opium quality.[192] The first of these suggests that opium use was prolific and was used to treat many ailments; the second illustrates a concern for the quality. This appears to be concerned mostly with the purchase of opium, but also relates to a need for safety where there is substantial difference in opioid concentration.[193]

The inclusion of very specific actions in relation to the harvest of poppy also indicates a concern for safety. An example is that the resin should be harvested at the third hour of the day.[194] This appears to be a social ritual, though precisely why it is useful is unclear. The regular application of opium in topical treatments is also a way of curbing the danger of the substance. It is only in a topical treatment where we find opium use in Soranus.[195] Additionally we find the use of less potent versions of poppy so as to protect the patients, particularly meconium, which consists of the boiled heads and leaves.[196] Thus this produces a weaker oral medicine making it appropriate for illnesses like sleeplessness without the risk of poisoning the user. Pliny also differentiates extensively between types of poppies and their different uses. This again is a means of allowing safe use both through the selection of a cultivar with known qualities and through assuring the patient that the poppy has known qualities and that it will be effective against the particular ailment.[197]

Elaterium was a Roman medicine made out of the juice of the seeds of the exploding cucumber.[198] As one can tell merely from that description, this substance is again associated with complex preparation. In contrast to others, however, it shows fewer signs of danger or restriction. In contrast, elaterium requires ageing to be effective, which would suggest usage mostly by professional healers.

---

[190] Pliny, *Naturalis Historiae*, 20.76. (App. 1: 1421);Pliny, *Naturalis Historiae*, 20.77. (App. 1: 1435).
[191] Pliny, *Naturalis Historiae*, 20.76. (App. 1: 1428).
[192] Pliny, *Naturalis Historiae*, 20.76. (App. 1: 1433).
[193] Frick, et al. (2005:666).
[194] Pliny, *Naturalis Historiae*, 20.76. (App. 1: 1420).
[195] Soranus, *Gynecology*, 3.31. (App. 1: 0379).
[196] Pliny, *Naturalis Historiae*, 20.76. (App. 1: 1432).
[197] Cf. Pliny, *Naturalis Historiae*, 20.76-79. (App. 1: 1419, 1420, 1434, 1436, 1440 and 1444.
[198] Exploding cucumber refers to *Ecballium elaterium* a plant native to Europe and northern Africa

As the instructions for making and ageing these lozenges are contained in medical texts it suggests that the physicians themselves were to make these products. As time was needed for their manufacture and they couldn't be made on demand it seems unlikely that a non-physician would keep a supply on hand. This would again be a remedy which would be difficult to produce as the quantities of juice yielded must have been low.[199] This again indicates it was likely applied mostly by physicians rather than the public which may explain the lack of controls. Pliny identifies that the lethal dose of elaterium or scorpion cucumber is greater than an obol.[200] We again see a reference to the testing of the substance to prove its quality, again an indication of possible danger. A particular time of year is also specified for the harvest and preparation of elaterium. This may either be a meaningless ritual or may be to encourage the standardisation of strength of the remedy.

Honey is among the most common of medicinals to appear in Roman treatments. It is most often not the active ingredient but just a component of mixtures. There are seemingly no restrictions on its use, including its regular use as food without medical implications.[201] It occurs regularly in all three works and is even given orally to infants.[202] This illustrates that it was not regarded as dangerous and so was also ascribed little power. The inclusion of honey in complex remedies is not an indication of an attempt to control risks as the honey does not appear as the main ingredient.

## 7 – How Romans Reduced the Danger of Medicines

From the treatments described in the ancient sources it is also possible to interpret what methods were used to regulate the use of dangerous treatments and medicine in general.

The first way patients were protected from pharmaceuticals was through a regulation of dose. An appropriate quantity of a treatment is often outlined in medical works, especially where the

---

[199] Pliny, *Naturalis Historiae*, 20.2.
[200] Pliny, *Naturalis Historiae*, 20.3. (App. 1: 0496); Scorpion cucumber is a wild Arabian variety of cucumber which is called cucumber by the general public. An associated living plant cannot be established. For a description see Pliny, *Naturalis Historiae*, XX. 3. 7-8.
[201] Soranus, *Gynecology*, 2.120, 3.13. (App. 1: 0197, 0113-0117); Pliny, *Naturalis Historiae*, 20.13, 20. 15, 20.17. (App. 1: 0577, 0579, 0601, 0616); Dioscorides, *De Materia Medica*, 1.1, 1.3, 1.13. (App. 1: 1717, 1719, 1731, 1778).
[202] Soranus, *Gynecology*, 2.86. (App. 1: 0085).

substance is regarded as dangerous.[203] It is surprising, however, that so many treatments do not list a quantity, suggesting that this feature was less significant than in our own society. This may well be explained as our medicines are precisely measured in relation to potency, whereas there would have been variation in the quality of the medicaments a Roman would use. This variation lends itself to a dynamic approach to the quantity of treatments and further illustrates the skills of Roman physicians.

A physician may also attempt to treat a disease with a substance of weaker potency.[204] This is well illustrated in the distinction between opium and meconium. Although they are seemingly applied to the same illnesses, the variation in strength allows for treating a patient with a reduced risk of death or gaining the stronger results from the more dangerous and potent treatment. In Dioscorides the use of other treatments of different strength is very common. Particularly it was widely believed that a 'wild' specimen was much more potent than its cultivated counterpart.[205] This may well be a reflection of the relative value of a wild specimen: if a treatment was more expensive due to it being drawn from wild plants, then the patient may expect stronger results.

A variation in the type of treatment can also be noted, particularly any movement away from treatments involving ingestion, as treatments become more dangerous. This of course reduces risk of poisoning and depending on the substance may have little to no effect on its efficacy. There was, with this method, a symbolic reduction in the effectiveness of the treatment with the same reduction applying to the risks. This particular tactic in reducing risk is also associated with those physicians who are less authoritative and more risky. This explains the polarisation of treatments in which women more commonly apply topical rather than oral treatments.

---

[203] E.g. Pliny, *Naturalis Historiae*, 20. 52, 20.78 . (App. 1: 1147, 1436).
[204] Soranus, *Gynecology*, 2.120. (App. 1: 0113), Pliny, *Naturalis Historiae*, 20.76. (App. 1: 1432).
[205] Dioscorides, *De Materia Medica*, 1.7.3. (App. 1: 1748) c.f. Dioscorides, *De Materia Medica*, 1.8.3. (App. 1: 1762).

Antidotes are also a common way of reducing the risk of dangerous substances. Mostly, where a dangerous treatment is listed, an antidote can also be found.[206] Entire works are dedicated to the listing of antidotes and by examining the pharmaceuticals in these antidotes it is clear that they would have been ineffective.[207] It was likely that they expected that antidotes would (rarely) actually save a person and, with this lack of confidence, they were not a principal means of promoting safe use of treatments but merely a last ditch attempt to prevent death.

Finally, as we have seen, a patient may use the expertise of a professional as a means of protecting themselves from harm. We see this in all sources whether explicit or implicit. In Soranus we have clear examples of the use of professional anointers, midwives and physicians.[208] This illustrates the distinction of their roles and shows how they would be utilised to perform specific treatments. In this respect we can expect that for many of the women's diseases a professional gynaecologist or midwife of either gender would likely have been sought to correctly treat the ailment.

## 8 – Conclusions

In this chapter it has been established that an understanding of Roman medicine from the Roman perspective can be best approximated through the use of numerous modern approaches. An understanding of the physical and social context of Roman healing illustrates that variations in healing locality were likely linked to gender roles. The social environment, too, was closely tied to gender and class and consequently illustrates major differences from the contemporary understanding of medicine. By analysing some language features we gained an understanding of the underlying meaning of terms, shedding light on Roman culture and its distinct approach to illness and medicine. A sample collection of treatments has also been assessed in relation to their danger and power in Roman healing. Such an analysis allows an understanding of the meanings ascribed to different objects and also forms a basis of further investigations. This process greatly benefitted from

---

[206] Pliny, *Naturalis Historiae*, 20.21, 34, 51,69 . (App. 1: 0697, 0876, 1082, 1315),Dioscorides, *De Materia Medica*, 1.19.4. (App. 1: 1828).
[207] Such as Nicander's *Alexipharmaca*.
[208] Soranus, *Gynecology*, 3.15. (App. 1: 0218); Soranus, *Gynecology*, 2.67, 3.32. (App. 1: 0058, 0304); Soranus, *Gynecology*, 4.9-10. (App. 1: 0448).

the understanding of gender as established in previous chapters. Using the data on the power of treatments a model was presented outlining the principle ways Roman culture regulated the risks of medicine.

# V – Conclusions

In the preceding work there have been many discoveries and highlights worthy of note, the foremost of which I will now present in conclusion.

By utilising a variety of non-traditional methods it became clear that the traditional view, presenting the *paterfamilias* as a healer, was in need of reassessment. While this may have represented an ideal, it failed to consider evidence showing that, in reality, a close involvement with medical treatment would often be unachievable due to the absence of the *paterfamilias*: these absences resulted from duties of the *paterfamilias* such as military service, management of rural properties, political or business obligations. It was also apparent that medicine should often be viewed as part of the domestic role. Evidence for this can be found in Celsus' reference to medicines kept 'on hand' and through the association with the domestic role in epigraphic material. Further, that as part of this role, it may have often been an activity for a woman, either a free matron or a slave, as in the case of a rural estate.[209]

It was also illustrated that, in contrast to republican sources and their modern proponents, the healer was a core aspect of medical treatment. This view was informed by the 'meaning response' and the universal tendency to place emphasis on the non-practical aspects of healing.[210] The clear statement of Pliny that, ideally, Romans should not place emphasis on the physicians also suggests that this was not the reality at the time. This established the importance of gender roles in healing as it showed that these positions would likely have been authoritative and represented a distinct part of female life.[211]

---

[209] This was identified based on associations within the epigraphic material, the instructions in the letters of Cicero and clear instructions in the agricultural manuals for the head slave's wife to be the medical carer.
[210] Moerman and Jonas (2002)
[211] That healers were significant demonstrates that the women fulfilling these roles should also not be taken lightly. Women fulfilling such roles can be seen in the *medicae* referred to in epigraphic material, the chief slave's wife found in the agricultural manuals and the midwives described in Soranus. Women who were members of a 'women's network' as discussed in Bailey (2012:5) were also examples of practitioners without having the same formal status.

Chapter II also established that women could be professional physicians.[212] This was achieved mostly using epigraphic material as evidence. The extent of their functions and their status in society were not clear from this evidence.

In contrast to the variety of sources used in chapter II, chapters III and IV drew their evidence from the material contained in appendix two and through comparison with social science methodologies and modern societies. In chapter III we found that medicines were burdened with social restrictions on their application. Most notably it was discovered that women tended to apply more topical treatments in comparison to orally administered pharmaceuticals. It appears that women did not perform surgery whereas men were not wetnurses and were likely to be less popular in the areas of midwifery and gynaecology.[213]

This distinction in medical practice was epitomised through the differences between Pliny and Soranus. While Pliny believed there were diseases particular to women this view was contradicted in Soranus' work. Similarly Pliny and Dioscorides make no mention of female healers while Soranus acknowledges them regularly despite preferring male practitioners. Soranus also ascribes greater rights to the patient than the earlier works. This was seen to fit with broader changes to the status of women in the society which occurred in this period.[214] This chapter also showed that female physicians must have possessed knowledge of medical theory. This was shown by the complex remedies found in Soranus, and furthered by his assertion that midwives required familiarity with medical literature. Through an understanding of how Romans perceived medicine this suggests that these women would have been capable to treat any form of disease not just those which effect women.

---

[212] Professional physicians were those performing this task as an occupation regardless of training as well as those who identified themselves with such an occupation i.e. call themselves doctors.

[213] This was shown based on comparison with Greek culture, particularly through mythology.

[214] The women of the ruling class were seen to be increasingly involved in public life. Examples were women such as Cornelia, Fulvia, Terentia, Antonia, Livia and Agrippina. It seems likely that this practice would then have filtered down to the rest of society. Additionally, there was a growth in the legal status of women in the empire. Particularly it was made easier for them to gain independence and hold property as shown by Gardner (1986) and Matthews (1995:767)

From the contrasts between Pliny and Soranus we also find that female physicians were likely well respected by the end of my period of study. There was resistance to referring to female healers in Pliny or Dioscorides while females are listed in a variety of roles in Soranus. They were, as expected, considered the leaders in the field of child birth and were notably given authority in regards to the decision of whether a child should be reared. This was established through the study of Soranus who identified female involvement early in his work; he later illustrates their role in advising the decision on the rearing of the child. The association of women with child birth is also established in artistic depictions. In this chapter the social status of female physicians was also explored, revealing that they, similar to their male counterparts, were often of low social status.[215] This was made clear through the use of epigraphy which showed that female physicians were often related to male physicians. The status of male physicians was, in turn, established jointly through their having either foreign or simple names (unlike the three names used by the elite) in epigraphy and through other sources, especially plays, which show that physicians were often foreigners and not of high social status. Through an examination of evidence from cultures similar to that of Rome it was also found that female healers were likely preferred by female patients, and that this practice was generally accepted by other male members of the household.[216]

Practices which excluded women were also considered.[217] This showed that while there were few practices which did not allow female involvement, there were notable differences in the ways in which medicine was practised. Surgery was an example of a form of treatment which excluded female practitioners. It was seen that this most likely stemmed from an inability to train them.[218]

---

[215] Physicians in the early Empire were traditionally of Greek origin and were often freedmen or the descendants of freedmen.
[216] From examination of "Greek" origins of female healers it was found that women likely preferred to have female medical attendants. The existence of female healers also suggests that they must have been preferred, since women in these roles were a contradiction of traditional gender roles in Roman society.
[217] The most notable excluded practice was surgery; this is suggested by the inability to train surgeons without war. Men were by necessity excluded from wet nursing and likely uncommon as midwives, as suggested in Soranus.
[218] The requirement to learn in battle situations was expressed in the pseudo-Hippocratic work *'The Physician'* thus precluding female involvement.

However, it was also suggested that this exclusion stemmed from a cultural concern that this occupation required skills unsuited or unbecoming of a woman.[219]

Chapter IV presented a framework, using modern approaches, to understand the significance of pharmaceuticals to a Roman and how Roman culture related to its medical system. It illustrated that the physical environment of medical treatment related to the gender of the practitioner and to the type and power of the treatment. This was achieved by examination of the treatment environments described in Soranus and examining how each space would affect a patient and the treatments possible. The social environment was also important; the gender and class of the physician having a notable impact on the form and effectiveness of treatment.[220] An assessment of the language used in Roman medicine also showed that it was a distinct medical system from its Greek and Italic predecessors. This was achieved by examining the meanings ascribed to Greek and Latin medical terms in order to understand the underlying cultural ideas behind these words. Using this framework a selection of treatments found in Roman medicine were considered and an attempt made to understand the power (by this I mean the perceived strength of a substance) and importance which was placed on them in Roman society. This investigation proved effective, though to apply this to a full set of treatments would be a mammoth task. Using this investigation a model was proposed which explained the ways in which Romans reduced the risks of pharmaceutical use.

Following on from this research there are a number of areas which would benefit from further study. As stated above an assessment of the power of more treatments would be an excellent area of research. Not only would this provide additional insight into Roman culture and medical treatments but the accuracy of the study would be improved through analysing more treatments thus providing more evidence. Although there is an apparent lack of evidence, greater research into the distinct role of female doctors, gynaecologists and midwives would be extremely valuable in terms of our

---

[219] The role of the surgeon involved an ability to ignore the pain of the patient. This would contrast with the expected role of a woman as a caring figure and so was culturally inappropriate.
[220] This was shown using conclusions drawn from throughout this thesis such as; the social class of the physician, the formality of the healer and the gender of the healer. The means of accessing medical care was also discussed as a substantial influence on the format of treatment.

understanding of these roles and women in professional healing. The use of innovative methodologies may allow for such an investigation.

Overall this work has revealed the complexities of gender and healing. It has shown that women were an active and integral part of Roman medicine and, through its attempt to reconstruct the Roman perspective, has returned a voice to the occupants of the ancient world.

# Bibliography

**Primary Sources**

Aulus Gellius in Gellius, A. (eds.), Rolfe, J. C. (trans.), (1982). *The Attic Nights of Aulus Gellius*. Cambridge

Cato *De Agricultura* in W. D. Hooper and H. B. Ash (eds.), (1934). *Cato, Varro. On Agriculture*. Cambrige Mass

Celsus *De Medicina* in W. G. Spencer (eds.), (1935). *On Medicine*. Harvard

Cicero, M. T. *Epistulae Ad Familiares* in Bailey, D. R. S. (eds.), (1966). *Letters to friends*. Harvard, London

Columella *De Re Rustica* in E. S. Forster and Edward H. Heffner (eds.), (1955). *On Agriculture: Books X - XII On Trees*. Harvard

Dioscorides *De Materia Medica* Beck, L. Y. (trans.), (2005). Hidesheim, Zurich, New York

Galen *De Praegnotione Ad Epigenem* in Nutton, V. (eds.), (1979). *Galeni De praecognitione, edidit, in linguam Anglicam vertit, commentatus est V. Nutton*. Berlin

Herodotus Ἱστορία in Godley, A. D. (eds.), (1971). *Herodotus: Histories*. London

Hippocrates *De Medico* in Coxe, J. R. (eds.), (1846). *The Writings of Hippocrates and Galen: Epitomised from the Original Latin translations*. Philadelphia

Hyginus *Fabula* in Rose, H. J. (eds.), (1934). *Hygini Fabulae*. Leiden

Lucian *Alexander* in A. M. Harmon (eds.), (1925). *Lucian: Anacharsis or Athletics. Menippus or The Descent into Hades. On Funerals. A Professor of Public Speaking. Alexander the False Prophet. Essays in Portraiture. Essays in Portraiture Defende. The Goddesse of Surrye*. Harverd

Maximus, V. *Factorum Ac Dictorum Memorabilium* in Bailey, D. R. S. (eds.), (2000). *Memorable Doings and Saying*. Cambridge Mass.

Plautus *Menaechmi* in Melo, W. d. (eds.), (2011). *Casina. The Casket Comedy. Curculio. Epidicus. The Two Menaechmuses*. Cambridge Mas.

Pliny *Naturalis Historiae* in Jones, W. H. S. (eds.), (1963). *Natural History*. Harvard

Pliny the Younger *Epistulae* in Radice, B. (eds.), (1969). *Letters*. Cambridge Mass.

Quintilian *Institutio Oratoria* in Donald A. Russell (eds.), (2002). *The Orator's Education: Books 1-2*. Harvard

Soranus *Gynecology* in Rose, V. (eds.), (1882). *Gynaeciorum vetus translatio latina*. Lipsiae

Soranus *Gynecology* Temkin, O. (trans.), (1956). *Soranus Gynecology*. Baltimore

Suetonius *Nero* in J.C. Rolfe (eds.), (1997). *Suetonius*. Cambride Mass

Tacitus *Dialogus De Oratoribus* in W. Peterson and M. Hutton (eds.), (1970). *Tacitus: Agricola, Germania, Dialogus*. Harvard

Tacitus *Annales* Woodman, A. J. (trans.), (2004). *The Annals*. Indianapolis

**Secondary Sources**

Abbott, M. E. S. (1911). *Women in Medicine*. Toronto.

Adcock, F. E. (1945). "Women in Roman Life and Letters." *Greece & Rome* 14: 1-11.

Allbutt, T. C. (1909). "The Fitzpatrick Lectures on Greek Medicine in Rome." *The British Medical Journal* 2: 1449-1455.

Allbutt, T. C. (1921). *Greek Medicine in Rome*. London.

Bailey, A. (2012). *Medicina Domestica: Medicine and Power in the Urban and Non-Urban Roman Household*, Australian National University.

Blackwell, B., Bloomfield, S. and Buncher, C. R. (1972). "Demonstration to Medical Students of Placebo Responses and Non-Drug Factors." *The Lancet* 299: 1279-1282.

Bliquez, L. J. (1981). "Greek and Roman Medicine: The Probing Surgical Tools of Antiquity." *Archaeology* 34: 10-17.

Bourdillon, H. (1988). *Women as Healers: A History of Women and Medicine*. Cambridge.

Bradley, K. (1986). 'Wet-Nursing at Rome: A Study in Social Relations'. in. Rawson, B. (eds.) *The Family in Ancient Rome: New Perspectives*. London, Sydney.

Branthwaite, A. and Cooper, P. (1981). "Analgesic Effects of Branding in Treatment of Headaches." *British Medical Journal (Clinical research ed.)* 282: 1576 - 1578.

Brillante, C. (1990). 'Myth and History'. in. Edmunds, L. (eds.) *Approaches to Greek Myth*. Baltimore.

Brumberg, J. J. (1997). 'The Appetite as Voice'. in. Counihan, C. and Van Esterik, P. (eds.) *Food and Culture: A Reader*. New York.

Cameron, A. and Kuhrt, A., (Eds.) (1987). *Images of Women in Antiquity*. London, Sydney.

Cattaneo, A., Lucchelli, P. and Filippucci, G. (1970). "Sedative Effects of Placebo Treatment." *European Journal of Clinical Pharmacology* 3: 43-45.

Clark, A. (1998). 'Magic Words: How Language Augments Human Computation'. in. Carruthers, P. and Boucher, J. (eds.) *Language and Thought: Interdisciplinary Themes*. Cambridge: 162-183.

Cushing, A. (1998). "Illness and Health in the Ancient World." *Collegian* 5: 44.

Deo, B. (2003). "Growing Saffron—the World's Most Expensive Spice." *Crop Food Research* 20: 1-4.

Dewitt, N. W. (1920). "The Primitive Roman Houshold." *The Classical Journal* 15: 216-225.

Dingwall, R., Rafferty, A. M. and Webster, C. (2002). *An Introduction to the Social History of Nursing*.

Douglas, M. (1997). 'Deciphering a Meal'. in. Counihan, C. and Van Esterik, P. (eds.) *Food and Culture: A Reader*. New York: 36-54.

Drabkin, I. E. (1944). "On Medical Education in Greece and Rome." *Bulletin of the History of Medicine* 15: 333-351.

Du Toit, B. M. (1997). *Drugs, Rituals and Altered States of Consciousness*. Rotterdam.

Dutton, D. L. (1988). "The Cold Reading Technique." *Experientia* 44: 326-332.

Edelstein, L. (1935). "The Development of Greek Anatomy." *Bulletin of the Institute of the History of Medicine* 3: 235-248.

Ehrenreich, B. and English, D. (2010). *Witches, Midwives, and Nurses: A History of Women Healers*. New York.

Everett, N. (2012). *The Alphabet of Galen: Pharmacy from Antiquity to the Middle Ages*. Toronto.

Fiddes, N. (1991). *Meat: A Natural Symbol*. London, New York.

Fieldhouse, P. (1986). *Food and Nutrition: Customs and Culture*. London.

Fischler, C. (1988). "Food, Self and Identity." *Social Science Information* 27: 275-292.

Flemming, R. (2000). *Medicine and the Making of Roman Women: Gender, Nature, and Authority from Celsus to Galen*. Oxford.

Flemming, R. (2007). "Women, Writing and Medicine in the Classical World." *The Classical Quarterly* 57: 257-279.

Frick, S., Kramell, R., Schmidt, J., Fist, A. J. and Kutchan, T. M. (2005). "Comparative Qualitative and Quantitative Determination of Alkaloids in Narcotic and Condiment Papaver Somniferum Cultivars." *Journal of Natural Products* 68: 666-673.

Gardner, J. F. (1986). *Women in Roman Law & Society*. London.

Gilman, S., King, H., Porter, R. and Rousseau, G. (1993). *Hysteria Beyond Freud*. Berkeley.

Glare, P. G. W. (2012). *Oxford Latin Dictionary*, Oxford.

Griffin, S. (1981). *Pornography and Silence: Culture's Revenge against Nature*. London.

Hemelrijk, E. A. (2004). "Masculinity and Femininity in the "Laudatio Turiae"." *The Classical Quarterly* 54: 185-197.

Hillman, D. C. A. (2004). *Representations of Pharmacy in Roman Literature from Cato to Ovid,* Ph.D. Thesis, The University of Wisconsin - Madison.

Hillman, D. C. A. (2008). *The Chemical Muse: Drug Use and the Roots of Western Civilization*.

Hopwood, B. L. (2004). *Heres Esto: Property, Dignity, and the Inheritance Rights of Roman Women 215 BC - AD 14,* Ph.D. Thesis, University of Sydney.

Jackson, R. (1988). *Doctors and Diseases in the Roman Empire*. Norman.

Joshel, S. R. (1986). "Nurturing the Master's Child: Slavery and the Roman Child-Nurse." *Signs* 12: 3-22.

Katz, P. (1999). *The Scalpel's Edge: The Culture of Surgeons*. Boston.

Keenan, M. (2004). 'The Social Context of Drug Use'. in. Hamilton, M. K., T. Ritter, A. (eds.) *Drug Use in Australia: Preventing Harm*. Oxford: 64 - 74.

King, H. (1986). "Agnodike and the Profession of Medicine." *The Cambridge Classical Journal (New Series)* 32: 53-77.

King, H. (1998). *Hyppocrates' Woman: Reading the Female Body in Ancient Greece*. London; New York.

King, H. (2005). *Health in Antiquity*. London.

King, H. (2007). *Midwifery, Obstetrics and the Rise of Gynaecology: The Uses of a Sixteenth-Century Compendium*. Aldershot.

Koloski-Ostrow, A. O. and Lyons, C. L., (Eds.) (1997). *Naked Truths: Women, Sexuality, and Gender in Classical Art and Archaeology*. London; New York.

Lakoff, G. and Johnson, M. (1980). *Metaphors We Live By*. Chicago.

Lawton, C. L. (2007). "Children in Classical Attic Votive Reliefs." *Hesperia Supplements* 41: 41-60.

Liddell, H. S., R. (2013). in Liddell, H. S., R., (Ed.)*An Intermediate Greek - English Lexicon,* New York.

Little, W., Fowler, H. and Coulson, J. (1973). in Onions, C. T., (Ed.)*The Shorter Oxford English Dictionary,* Oxford, Vol. 1.

MacMullen, R. (1980). "Women in Public in the Roman Empire." *Historia: Zeitschrift für Alte Geschichte* 29: 208-218.

Majno, G. (1975). *The Healing Hand: Man and Wound in the Ancient World*. Cambridge Mass.

Mariani-Costantini, R., Catalano, P., di Gennaro, F., di Tota, G. and Angeletti, L. R. (2000). "New Light on Cranial Surgery in Ancient Rome." *The Lancet* 355: 305-307.

Matthews, J. (1995). 'Roman Life and Society'. in. Boardman, J. G., J. Murray, O. (eds.) *The Oxford History of the Classical World*. Oxford.

Mead, M. (1937). *Cooperation and Competition Amoung Primitive Peoples*. New York.

Meigs, A. (1997). 'Food as Cultural Construction'. in. C. Counihan, P. V. E. (eds.) *Food and Culture: A Reader*. London.

Moerman, D. E. and Jonas, W. B. (2002). "Deconstructing the Placebo Effect and Finding the Meaning Response." *Annals of Internal Medicine* 136: 471 - 476.

Monaghan, J. and Just, P. (2000). *Social and Cultural Anthropology: A Very Short Introduction*. Oxford.

Moore, D. (1993). "Social Controls, Harm Minimisation and Interactive Outreach: The Public Health Implications of an Ethnography of Drug Use." *Australian Journal of Public Health* 17: 58-67.

Murphy, T. M. (2004). *Pliny the Elder's Natural History: The Empire in the Encyclopedia*. Oxford, New York.

Nickel, D. (1979). "Berufsvorstellungen Über Weibliche Medizinal-Personen in Der Antike." *Klio* 61: 515.

Nutting, M. A. (1907). *A History of Nursing; the Evolution of Nursing Systems from the Earliest Times to the Foundation of the First English and American Training Schools for Nurses.* New York; London.

Nutton, V. (1985). "The Drug Trade in Antiquity." *Journal of the Royal Society of Medicine* 78: 138-145.

Nutton, V. (1986). 'The Perils of Patriotism: Pliny and Roman Medicine'. in. French, R. and Greenaway, F. (eds.) *Science in the Early Roman Empire.* London.

Nutton, V. (2004). *Ancient Medicine.* London.

Parker, H. N. (1997). 'Women Doctors in Greece, Rome and the Byzantine Empire'. in. Furst, L. R. (eds.) *Women Physicians and Healers: Climbing a Long Hill.* Lexington.

Pinkster, H. (1992). "Notes on the Syntax of Celsus." *Mnemosyne* 45: 513-524.

Poblome, J. (2004). "Comparing Ordinary Craft Production: Textile and Pottery Production in Roman Asia Minor." *Journal of the Economic and Social History of the Orient* 47: 491 - 506.

Powell, B. B. (2009). *Classical Myth.* New York.

Rawson, B. (1986). 'The Roman Family'. in. Rawson, B. (eds.) *The Family in Ancient Rome.* Sydney.

Rawson, B. (2003). *Children and Childhood in Roman Italy.* Oxford.

Retief, F. P. and Cilliers, L. (2006). "The Healing Hand: The Role of Women in Graeco-Roman Medicine." *Acta Theologica* 26: 165-188.

Rivers, W. H. R. (1927). *Medicine, Magic, and Religion.* London.

Rubin, M. (2008). "Cultural History I: What's in a Name?" on The Institute of Historical Research *Making History: The changing face of the profession in Britain* Retrieved 6/5/15, from http://www.history.ac.uk/makinghistory/resources/articles/cultural_history.html.

Scarborough, J. (1969). *Roman Medicine.* London.

Scarborough, J. (1970). "Romans and Physicians." *The Classical Journal* 65: 296-306.

Scarborough, J. (1986). 'Pharmacy in Pliny's Natural History: Some Observations on Substances and Sources'. in. R. French and F. Greenaway (eds.) *Science in the Early Roman Empire: Pliny the Elder, His Sources and Influence.* London: 59-85.

Scarborough, J. (1993). 'Roman Medicine to Galen'. in. (eds.) *Aufstieg Und Niedergang Der Romischen Welt.* Berlin.

Schapira, K., McClelland, H., Griffiths, N. and Newell, D. (1970). "Study on the Effects of Tablet Colour in the Treatment of Anxiety States." *British Medical Journal* 2: 446 - 449.

Schulz, F. (1951). *Classical Roman Law.* Oxford.

Scullard, H. H. (2009). *From the Gracchi to Nero: A History of Rome from 133 BC to AD 68.* London.

Singer, M. and Baer, H. (2012). *Introducing Medical Anthropology: A Dicipline in Action.* Lanham.

Temkin, O. (1956). *Soranus Gynecology.* Baltimore.

University of Virginia. (2007). "The Doctor in Roman Society." on *Historical Collections at the Claude Moore Health Sciences Library* Retrieved 25/9/15, from http://exhibits.hsl.virginia.edu/antiqua/doctors/.

Watters, E. (2010) "The Americanization of Mental Illness" *The New York Times* 13 October http://www.nytimes.com/2010/01/10/magazine/10psyche-t.html?_r=2&pagewanted=print[10/13/2010&.

Weckowicz, T. E. and Liebel-Weckowicz, H. P. (1990). *A History of Great Ideas in Abnormal Psychology*. Amsterdam.

Weil, A. (1998). *The Natural Mind: An Investigation of Drugs and the Higher Consciousness*. Boston.

Zinberg, N. E. (1984). *Drug, Set and Setting: The Basis for Controlled Intoxicant Use*. New Haven, London.

**Appendix 1 – Roman Remedies Surveyed**

| n# | Reference | Treatment | Type | Aim (illness) |
|---|---|---|---|---|
| 0001 | Sor. 1. 26 | Warm oil vaginal suppository | v. sup. | First menstruation |
| 0002 | Sor. 1. 26 | Rest and bathing | bath | First menstruation |
| 0003 | Sor. 1. 26 | Moderate rocking and walking | other | First menstruation |
| 0004 | Sor. 1. 26 | Softening medicines suppositories and injections | v. sup. | First menstruation |
| 0005 | Sor. 1. 49 | Vigorous rubbing | bath | Pica pregnancy (2nd Trimester) |
| 0006 | Sor. 1. 50 | Cupping | cupping | Pica pregnancy (2nd Trimester) |
| 0007 | Sor. 1. 51 | Dietary remedies | oral | Pica pregnancy (2nd Trimester) |
| 0008 | sor. 1. 54 | Exercise sleep vocal exercises | other | Pregnancy (3rd Trimester) |
| 0009 | Sor. 1. 56 | Hold abdomen up with bandages | other | Pregnancy (3rd Trimester) |
| 0010 | Sor. 1. 56 | Rub abdomen with oil | bath | Pregnancy (3rd Trimester) |
| 0011 | Sor. 1. 56 | Lots of vaginal suppositories and dilating the uterus | v. sup. | Pregnancy (3rd Trimester) |
| 0012 | Sor. 1. 61 | Apply sticky things, lead or wool to the vagina | topical | Contraception |
| 0013 | Sor. 1. 61 | Woman hold breath and draw away | other | Contraception |
| 0014 | Sor. 1. 61 | Squat and induce sneezing, wipe vagina | other | Contraception |
| 0015 | Sor. 1. 61 | Smear cervix with old olive oil | topical | Contraception |
| 0016 | Sor. 1. 61 | Smear cervix with honey | topical | Contraception |
| 0017 | Sor. 1. 61 | Smear cervix with cedar resin | topical | Contraception |
| 0018 | Sor. 1. 61 | Smear cervix with juice of the balsam tree | topical | Contraception |
| 0019 | Sor. 1. 61 | Smear cervix with white lead with other things | topical | Contraception |
| 0020 | Sor. 1. 61 | Smear cervix with myrtle oil and white lead | topical | Contraception |
| 0021 | Sor. 1. 61 | Smear cervix with moist alum | topical | Contraception |
| 0022 | Sor. 1. 61 | Smear cervix with galbanum and wine | topical | Contraception |
| 0023 | Sor. 1. 61 | Put a lock of fine wool on cervix | v. sup. | Contraception |
| 0024 | Sor. 1. 61 | Vaginal suppositories to contract and condense | v. sup. | Contraception |
| 0025 | Sor. 1. 62 | Pine bark, Tanning sumach, equal w/ wine wrapped in wool | v. sup. | Contraception |

| | | | | |
|---|---|---|---|---|
| 0026 | Sor. 1. 62 | Cimolian earth, panax root, equal w/ water wrapped in wool | v. sup. | Contraception |
| 0027 | Sor. 1. 62 | Inside pomegranate peel w/ water | v. sup. | Contraception |
| 0028 | Sor. 1. 62 | 2 pomegranate peels, 1 oak galls after menstruation | v. sup. | Contraception |
| 0029 | Sor. 1. 62 | Moist alum, inside pomegranate rind w/ water app/ wool | v. sup. | Contraception |
| 0030 | Sor. 1. 62 | Unripe oak galls, outside pomegranate peel, ginger (2dracmas) w/ wine and dry | v. sup. | Contraception |
| 0031 | Sor. 1. 62 | Grind figs and Natron | v. sup. | Contraception |
| 0032 | Sor. 1. 62 | Pomegranate peel, gum and oil of roses | v. sup. | Contraception |
| 0033 | Sor. 1. 62 | Honey water | v. sup. | Contraception |
| 0034 | Sor. 1. 63 | Cyrenaic Balm w/ 2 cyaths of water | drink | Induce menstruation (contraception)(abortion) |
| 0035 | Sor. 1. 63 | Wallflower seed, myrtle (3obles each), Myrrh (1drachm), white pepper 2 seeds w/ wine (3days) | drink | Induce menstruation (contraception)(abortion) |
| 0036 | Sor. 1. 63 | Rocket seed (1obol), cow parsnip (1/2 Obol) w/ oxymel | drink | Induce menstruation (contraception)(abortion) |
| 0037 | Sor. 1. 63 | Amulets | folk | Induce menstruation (contraception)(abortion) |
| 0038 | Sor. 1. 63 | Mule uteri and ear dirt | folk | Induce menstruation (contraception)(abortion) |
| 0039 | Sor. 1. 63 | Panax balm, Cyrenaic Balm and Rue seeds (2 obols) coat with wax w/ diluted wine | oral | Induce menstruation (contraception)(abortion) |
| 0040 | Sor. 1. 64 | Old oil | injection | Abortive |
| 0041 | Sor. 1. 64 | Old oil W/ rue juice or honey or iris oil or absenthium & honey or panax balm or spelt, rue and honey or Syrian Unguent | injection | Abortive |
| 0042 | Sor. 1. 64 | Poultice and plasters of lupine meal, ox bile and absenthium | poultice and plaster | Abortive |
| 0043 | Sor. 1. 64 | Heavy exercise shaking etc. (for 30 days) | other | Abortive |
| 0044 | Sor. 1. 64 | Diuretics (to bring about menstruation) | oral | Abortive |
| 0045 | Sor. 1. 64 | Rubbing w/ oils | bath | Abortive |
| 0046 | Sor. 1. 64 | Hot baths | bath | Abortive |
| 0047 | Sor. 1. 64 | Oil suppositories | v. sup. | Abortive |

| | | | | |
|---|---|---|---|---|
| 0048 | Sor. 1. 64 | Bath of linseed, fenugreek, mallow, marshmallow and wormwood | bath | Abortive |
| 0049 | Sor. 1. 64 | Poultice of linseed, fenugreek, mallow, marshmallow and wormwood | poultice | Abortive |
| 0050 | Sor. 1. 65 | Softening vaginal suppositories | v. sup. | Pre abortive |
| 0051 | Sor. 1. 65 | Myrtle, wallflower seed, bitter lupines (equal) /w water | v. sup. | Abortive |
| 0052 | Sor. 1. 65 | Rue leaves (3drachms), myrtle (2 drachms) and sweet bay (2 drachms) w/ wine | v. sup. | Abortive |
| 0053 | Sor. 1. 65 | Wallflower, cardamom, brimstone, absenthium, myrrh (equal) w/ water | v. sup. | Abortive |
| 0054 | Sor. 1. 65 | Bleed a lot | venesection | Abortive |
| 0055 | Sor. 1. 65 | No wine | oral | Pre abortive |
| 0056 | Sor. 1. 65 | Shacking | other | Abortive |
| 0057 | Sor. 1. 65 | Softening clyster | topical | Abortive |
| 0058 | Sor. 2. 67 (2) | Pennyroyal, clod of earth, barley groats, apple, quince, lemon, melon and cucumber | smelling | Birth (revival) |
| 0059 | Sor. 2. 68 | Winching out foetus | other | Difficult birth |
| 0060 | Sor. 2. 69 | Warm oil (lots) | topical | Birth (revival) |
| 0061 | sor. 2. 69 | Worm oil soaked cloths on abdomen | topical | Birth (revival) |
| 0062 | Sor. 2. 76 | Sea sponge and diluted vinegar | topical | Inflamed breasts |
| 0063 | Sor. 2. 76 | Alum or fleawort and coriander or purslane | topical | Stop lactation |
| 0064 | Sor. 2. 76 | Relaxing poultices bread softened by water and olive oil or hydromel | poultice | Tension or clotting of breasts |
| 0065 | Sor. 2. 76 | Fomentations and warm oil squeezed with sponges w/warm water or fenugreek, mallow, or linseed | bath | Tension or clotting of breasts |
| 0066 | Sor. 2. 76 | Surgery | surgery | Suppurating breasts |
| 0067 | Sor. 2. 76 | Wax salve | salve | Breast inflammations past its height |
| 0068 | Sor. 2. 77 | Ground pyrite | poultice | Stopping lactation |
| 0069 | Sor. 2. 77 | Cypress, wine and saffron | poultice | Stopping lactation |
| 0070 | Sor. 2. 77 | Henna oil, triturated pumice | poultice | Stopping lactation |
| 0071 | Sor. 2. 77 | Cumin W/ oil or water | poultice | Stopping lactation |

| | | | | |
|---|---|---|---|---|
| 0072 | Sor. 2. 77 | Moist alum w/ vinegar and rose oil | poultice | Stopping lactation |
| 0073 | Sor. 2. 77 | Cumin, raisins | poultice | Stopping lactation |
| 0074 | Sor. 2. 77 | Sesame w/ honey | poultice | Stopping lactation |
| 0075 | Sor. 2. 77 | Green tribulus boiled in Vinegar | poultice | Stopping lactation |
| 0076 | Sor. 2. 77 | Ivy b in Vinegar | poultice | Stopping lactation |
| 0077 | Sor. 2. 77 | Dried figs b. In Vinegar | poultice | Stopping lactation |
| 0078 | Sor. 2. 77 | Bran b. In Vinegar | poultice | Stopping lactation |
| 0079 | Sor. 2. 77 | Celery w/ bread | poultice | Stopping lactation |
| 0080 | Sor. 2. 77 | Peppermint w/ bread | poultice | Stopping lactation |
| 0081 | Sor. 2. 77 | Cabbage w/ bread | poultice | Stopping lactation |
| 0082 | Sor. 2. 80 | Use of anything sharp (including bread) | surgery | Omphalectomy |
| 0083 | Sor. 2. 82 | Sprinkle with fine salt, natron or aphronitre (possibly diluted) | bath | Clean and firm up flesh (newborn) |
| 0084 | Sor. 2. 82 | Clean eyes with oil | bath | Newborn |
| 0085 | sor. 2. 86 | Give baby honey and hydromel | oral | Newborn |
| 0086 | Sor. 2. 87 | Use wet-nurse for at least 3 days | other | |
| 0087 | Sor. 2. 95 | Nurse to wean herself onto wine after 40 days | diet | |
| 0088 | Sor. 2. 97 | Relaxing exercise, walks and rubbing especially breasts | other | To prevent lactation stopping |
| 0089 | Sor. 2. 97 | Vocal exercises, baths, wholesome foods and upper exercises | other | To prevent lactation stopping |
| 0090 | Sor. 2. 98 | Vigorous exercise | other | Lessen milk production |
| 0091 | Sor. 2. 98 | Baths, eat gruel like foods and drink water | diet | Make milk more liquid |
| 0092 | Sor. 2. 98 | Far or spelt porridge, eggs, pine cones, pigs feet, snouts and ears, meat of kids and some wine | diet | Thicken milk |
| 0093 | Sor. 2. 110 | Ground pig ankle bone | powder topical | Healing the navel |
| 0094 | Sor. 2. 110 | Ground snail shell | powder topical | Healing the navel |
| 0095 | Sor. 2. 110 | Bulb of purse tassels | powder | Healing the navel |

| | | | | |
|---|---|---|---|---|
| 0096 | Sor. 2. 110 | Heated lead | topical | Healing the navel |
| 0097 | Sor. 2. 118 | Chicken fat | topical | Softening gums (teething) |
| 0098 | Sor. 2. 118 | Hare brain | bath | Softening gums (teething) |
| 0099 | Sor. 2. 118 | Oil soaked wool on neck hands and jaws | topical | Softening gums (teething) |
| 0100 | Sor. 2. 118 | Meal | poultices | Softening gums (teething) |
| 0101 | Sor. 2. 118 | Fenugreek | poultices | Softening gums (teething) |
| 0102 | Sor. 2. 118 | Linseed | poultices | Softening gums (teething) |
| 0103 | Sor. 2. 118 | Sea sponge w/ boiled honey | fomentation | Softening gums (teething) |
| 0104 | Sor. 2. 118 | No bath wet nurse to drink little (only water) and gruel like food and should force milk from the breast | oral | Sympathetic disturbances |
| 0105 | Sor. 2. 119 | Sea sponge w/ honey water and juice of barley | oral | Inflamed tonsils |
| 0106 | Sor. 2. 119 | Hot cumin w/ water poultice and salt w/ olive oil on tonsils + ritual | oral | Inflamed tonsils |
| 0107 | Sor. 2. 120 | Honey (if small) | oral | Oral thrush |
| 0108 | Sor. 2. 120 | Loosening poultice (if dry and inflamed) | oral | Oral thrush |
| 0109 | Sor. 2. 120 | Astringent poultice, lentils and pomegranate peel (if moist) | oral | Oral thrush |
| 0110 | Sor. 2. 120 | Anthera remedy | oral | Oral thrush |
| 0111 | Sor. 2. 120 | Rose of cypress blossom | oral | Oral thrush |
| 0112 | Sor. 2. 120 | Tamarisk fruit | oral | Oral thrush |
| 0113 | Sor. 2. 120 | Black mulberries, poppyheads and plantain w/ honey (when healing) | oral | Oral thrush |
| 0114 | Sor. 2. 120 | Other astringent w/ honey (when healing) | oral | Oral thrush |
| 0115 | Sor. 2. 120 | Iris w/ honey or dry powder | oral | Oral thrush |
| 0116 | Sor. 2. 120 | Rose leaves chopped, rose blossom, saffron, myrrh, oak gall, frankincense, frankincense bark w/ honey | oral | Oral thrush |
| 0117 | Sor. 2. 120 | Honey water and the juice of a sweet pomegranate | oral | Oral thrush |
| 0118 | Sor. 2. 121 | Heat | bath | Itching |

| | | | | |
|---|---|---|---|---|
| 0119 | Sor. 2. 121 | Olive oil and wax | bath | Itching |
| 0120 | Sor. 2. 121 | Bathing w/ roses or lentils (when eruptions at height) | bath | Exanthemata, blisters and sores |
| 0121 | Sor. 2. 121 | Bathing w/ myrtle, mastic, bramble or pomegranate peel (when eruptions at height) more astringent | bath | Exanthemata, blisters and sores at height |
| 0122 | Sor. 2. 121 | Plantain w/ bread | poultice | Exanthemata, blisters and sores at height |
| 0123 | Sor. 2. 121 | Endive | poultice | Exanthemata, blisters and sores at height |
| 0124 | Sor. 2. 121 | Powder of barley and purslane | poultice | Exanthemata, blisters and sores at height |
| 0125 | Sor. 2. 121 | Houseleek | poultice | Exanthemata, blisters and sores at height |
| 0126 | Sor. 2. 121 | Navelwort | poultice | Exanthemata, blisters and sores at height |
| 0127 | Sor. 2. 121 | Dried roses | poultice | Exanthemata, blisters and sores at height |
| 0128 | Sor. 2. 121 | Fresh roses boiled with melilot or dates | poultice | Exanthemata, blisters and sores at height |
| 0129 | Sor. 2. 121 | Litharge, white lead, alum, vinegar, w/ myrtle oil or rose oil or mastic oil | ointment | Exanthemata, blisters and sores at height |
| 0130 | Sor. 2. 122 | Water and olive oil (when over peek) | bath | Exanthemata, blisters and sores over peak |
| 0131 | Sor. 2. 122 | Linseed | bath | Exanthemata, blisters and sores over peak |
| 0132 | Sor. 2. 122 | Fenugreek | bath | Exanthemata, blisters and sores over peak |
| 0133 | Sor. 2. 122 | Roots of wild mallow | bath | Exanthemata, blisters and sores over peak |
| 0134 | Sor. 2. 122 | Egg white with moist wax salve | salve | Exanthemata, blisters and sores over peak |
| 0135 | Sor. 2. 122 | Boiled honey | salve | Exanthemata, blisters and sores over peak |
| 0136 | Sor. 2. 122 | Lentils with boiled | salve | Exanthemata, blisters and sores over peak |
| 0137 | Sor. 2. 122 | White lead | topical | On clean ulcer to seal it |
| 0138 | Sor. 2. 122 | The remedy diluted with juices | topical | On clean ulcer to seal it |
| 0139 | Sor. 2. 122 | Gum laudanum | poultice | On clean ulcer to seal it |
| 0140 | Sor. 2. 122 | Eggs | poultice | On clean ulcer to seal it |
| 0141 | Sor. 2. 122 | Barleycorn | poultice | On clean ulcer to seal it |
| 0142 | Sor. 2. 122 | Cadmia w/ rose oil | poultice | On clean ulcer to seal it |

| | | | | |
|---|---|---|---|---|
| 0143 | Sor. 2. 122 | Cleans with natron | bath | On clean ulcer to seal it |
| 0144 | Sor. 2. 122 | Sweet diet for nurse | diet | On clean ulcer to seal it |
| 0145 | Sor. 2. 122 | Honey suppository | suppository | To make bowels move |
| 0146 | Sor. 2. 122 | Turpentine suppository to size of chickpea | suppository | To make bowels move |
| 0147 | Sor. 2. 122 | Millet | oral? | Loose bowels |
| 0148 | Sor. 2. 123 | Cardamom, cumin, nettle seed and pepper | lozenge | Wheezing |
| 0149 | Sor. 2. 123 | Honey water | oral | Wheezing |
| 0150 | Sor. 2. 123 | Induce vomiting | other | Swallowed phlegm |
| 0151 | Sor. 2. 123 | Small pine cone, roasted almonds, linseed, juice of liquorice, pine seed, tragacanth and honey | lozenge | Coughing |
| 0152 | Sor. 2. 124 | Egg yolk w/ rose oil | pledget | Psoriasis |
| 0153 | Sor. 2. 124 | Heliotrope leaf, grated pumpkin, melon skin, juice of black nightshade, w/ rose oil | pledget | Psoriasis |
| 0154 | Sor. 2. 125 | Omit bathing and passive exercise | bath | Flux of the bowels |
| 0155 | Sor. 2. 125 | Astringent plasters | plaster | Flux of the bowels |
| 0156 | Sor. 2. 125 | Inject juice of plantain (1/2 pint) w/ ear syringe | injection | Flux of the bowels |
| 0157 | Sor. 2. 125 | Nurse to receive equivalent treatment (no bath astringent food and water) | bath, oral | Flux of the bowels |
| 0158 | Sor. 3. 9 | Cut away hymen | surgery | Disease preventing menstrual flux |
| 0159 | Sor. 3. 9 | Massage uterus | other | Disease preventing menstrual flux |
| 0160 | Sor. 3. 9 | Treat uterus with hardening medicines | topical | Disease preventing menstrual flux |
| 0161 | Sor. 3. 10 | Put in a warm light room and apply pressure to parts in pain | other | Disease preventing menstrual flux |
| 0162 | Sor. 3. 10 | Warm cloth | fomentation | Full retention of menstrual flux |
| 0163 | Sor. 3. 10 | Warm linen towels w/ wool and warming pans filled with warm water | other | Full retention of menstrual flux |
| 0164 | Sor. 3. 10 | Bladders containing warm oil | topical | Full retention of menstrual flux |
| 0165 | Sor. 3. 10 | Lukewarm ground grain in bags | topical | Full retention of menstrual flux |
| 0166 | Sor. 3. 10 | Sponge wrung out in boiling water and wrapped in cloth | topical | Full retention of menstrual flux |

| ID | Source | Treatment | Method | Condition |
|---|---|---|---|---|
| 0167 | Sor. 3. 10 | Soft wool in oil applied to loins and abdomen | topical | Full retention of menstrual flux |
| 0168 | Sor. 3. 10 | Warm water as mouthwash and to drink | oral | Full retention of menstrual flux |
| 0169 | Sor. 3. 10 | Linseed | poultices | Full retention of menstrual flux |
| 0170 | Sor. 3. 10 | Bread w/ warm hydromel | poultices | Full retention of menstrual flux |
| 0171 | Sor. 3. 10 | Sitz baths | bath | Full retention of menstrual flux |
| 0172 | Sor. 3. 10 | Rubdown with ointment | topical | Full retention of menstrual flux |
| 0173 | Sor. 3. 11 | Venesection behind arm | venesection | Full retention of menstrual flux |
| 0174 | Sor. 3. 11 | Warm oil with water (Sitz bath) | bath | Full retention of menstrual flux |
| 0175 | Sor. 3. 11 | Fenugreek, linseed and mallow (Sitz bath) | bath | Full retention of menstrual flux |
| 0176 | Sor. 3. 11 | Fenugreek, linseed and mallow w/ egg mix | poured into labia (injection) | Full retention of menstrual flux |
| 0177 | Sor. 3. 11 | Wool soaked in fenugreek, linseed and mallow w/ egg mix surrounded by felt | v. sup. | Full retention of menstrual flux |
| 0178 | Sor. 3. 11 | Warm water as mouthwash and to drink | oral | Full retention of menstrual flux |
| 0179 | Sor. 3. 11 | Spelt gruel w/ honey water or water | oral | Full retention of menstrual flux |
| 0180 | Sor. 3. 11 | Gruel w/ honey | oral | Full retention of menstrual flux |
| 0181 | Sor. 3. 11 | Gruel w/ olive oil dill and salt | oral | Full retention of menstrual flux |
| 0182 | Sor. 3. 11 | Gruel w/ soaked bread | oral | Full retention of menstrual flux |
| 0183 | Sor. 3. 11 | Gruel w/ sipping eggs | oral | Full retention of menstrual flux |
| 0184 | Sor. 3. 11 | Give food only every second day | oral | Full retention of menstrual flux |
| 0185 | Sor. 3. 11 | Cupping dry followed by wet | cupping | Full retention of menstrual flux (3rd day after venesection) |
| 0186 | Sor. 3. 11 | Wet cupping of pubes and hypochondriac region | cupping | Full ret. of menstrual Flux (ailment at height initial stage abating) |
| 0187 | Sor. 3. 11 | Use leeches if above ineffective | cupping | Full ret. of menstrual Flux (ailment at height initial stage abating) |

| | | | | | |
|---|---|---|---|---|---|
| 0188 | Sor. 3. 11 | Relaxing poultices bread w/ warm pork fat | poultices | Healing leech wounds | |
| 0189 | Sor. 3. 11 | Relaxing poultices bread boiled w/ wild marrow root | poultices | Healing leech wounds | |
| 0190 | Sor. 3. 11 | Relaxing poultices bread boiled w/ linseed w/ the finest meal | poultices | Healing leech wounds | |
| 0191 | Sor. 3. 11 | Relaxing poultices bread boiled w/ fenugreek | poultices | Healing leech wounds | |
| 0192 | Sor. 3. 11 | Relaxing poultices bread boiled with olive oil honey and a decoction of mallow or fenugreek | poultices | Healing leech wounds | |
| 0193 | Sor. 3. 11 | Warm oil anal injection (4 cyaths) | injection | Full retention of menstrual flux | |
| 0194 | Sor. 3. 11 | Simple anal suppositories | suppository | Full retention of menstrual flux | |
| 0195 | Sor. 3. 13 | Wool w/ warm olive oil | suppository | Full retention of menstrual flux | |
| 0196 | Sor. 3. 13 | Juice of fenugreek, linseed or mallow beaten in oil and boiled with goose or chicken fat on wool | suppository | Full retention of menstrual flux | |
| 0197 | Sor. 3. 13 | 196 triturated with egg yolk by means of refined honey | suppository | Full retention of menstrual flux | |
| 0198 | Sor. 3. 13 | Melilot in sweet wine | decoction | Full retention of menstrual flux | |
| 0199 | Sor. 3. 13 | Inner part of dates boiled with sweet wine | oral | Full retention of menstrual flux | |
| 0200 | Sor. 3. 13 | Sponges w/ hot water | topical | Full retention of menstrual flux | |
| 0201 | Sor. 3. 13 | Sponges w/ oil and hot water | topical | Full retention of menstrual flux | |
| 0202 | Sor. 3. 13 | Sponges with fenugreek, linseed or mallow decoction, swinging in hammock | topical, other | Full ret. of menstrual Flux when progressed well | |
| 0203 | Sor. 3. 14 | Bathing | bath | Full ret. of mens. Flux when healed (restoratives) | |
| 0204 | Sor. 3. 14 | Varied food | diet | Full ret. of mens. Flux when healed (restoratives) | |
| 0205 | Sor. 3. 14 | Wine | diet | Full ret. of mens. Flux when healed (restoratives) | |
| 0206 | Sor. 3. 14 | Rocking | other | Full ret. of mens. Flux when healed (restoratives) | |
| 0207 | Sor. 3. 14 | Promenading | other | Full ret. of mens. Flux when healed (restoratives) | |
| 0208 | Sor. 3. 14 | Active exercises | other | Full ret. of mens. Flux when healed (restoratives) | |
| 0209 | Sor. 3. 14 | Massage of the whole body | other | Full ret. of mens. Flux when healed (restoratives) | |
| 0210 | Sor. 3. 14 | Massage uterus w/ sponges | topical | Full ret. of mens. Flux when healed (restoratives) | |
| 0211 | Sor. 3. 14 | Marjoram or lily oil smeared on orifice and neck of uterus | cerates | Full ret. of mens. Flux when healed (restoratives) | |

| | | | | |
|---|---|---|---|---|
| 0212 | Sor. 3. 14 | High emollient suppositories: wax, turpentine, ox fat w/ olive or henna oil | bath | Full ret. of mens. Flux when healed (restoratives) |
| 0213 | Sor. 3. 14 | Suppository of juices | suppository | Full ret. of mens. Flux when healed (restoratives) |
| 0214 | Sor. 3. 14 | Marrow, fat, and relaxing seed | suppository | Full ret. of mens. Flux when healed (restoratives) |
| 0215 | Sor. 3. 14 | Marjoram remedy for the relief of pain | | Full ret. of mens. Flux when healed (restoratives) |
| 0216 | Sor. 3. 14 | Olive oil | bath | Full ret. of mens. Flux when healed (restoratives) |
| 0217 | Sor. 3. 15 | If chronic use treatments during attacks and then restoratives | other | Full ret. of mens. Flux chronic |
| 0218 | Sor. 3. 15 | Use a professional anointer | bath | Full ret. of mens. Flux chronic |
| 0219 | Sor. 3. 15 | Metasyncretic cure | diet | Full ret. of mens. Flux chronic |
| 0220 | Sor. 3. 15 | Fasting followed by bread diet w/pungent | diet | Full ret. of mens. Flux chronic |
| 0221 | Sor. 3. 15 | Then the bland foods vegetables brain or delicate fish | diet | Full ret. of mens. Flux chronic |
| 0222 | Sor. 3. 15 | Then to fowl | diet | Full ret. of mens. Flux chronic |
| 0223 | Sor. 3. 15 | Then to fresh pork | diet | Full ret. of mens. Flux chronic |
| 0224 | Sor. 3. 15 | No wine or bath on the day of the change but both the day after | diet | Full ret. of mens. Flux chronic |
| 0225 | Sor. 3. 15 | Also apply topical remedies like above after the pungent period | diet | Full ret. of mens. Flux chronic |
| 0226 | Sor. 3. 15 | Then repeat but induce vomiting in addition to the fast with radishes | diet | Full ret. of mens. Flux chronic |
| 0227 | Sor. 3. 16 | Irritating cataplasms: bayberries | poultice | Full ret. of mens. Flux chronic |
| 0228 | Sor. 3. 16 | Irritating cataplasms: seeds | poultice | Full ret. of mens. Flux chronic |
| 0229 | Sor. 3. 16 | Irritating suppositories: rue ground w/ honey | v. sup. | Full ret. of mens. Flux chronic |
| 0230 | Sor. 3. 16 | Irritating suppositories: thin leaved fleabane | v. sup. | Full ret. of mens. Flux chronic |
| 0231 | Sor. 3. 16 | Irritating suppositories: raisons without stones w/ natron or salt | v. sup. | Full ret. of mens. Flux chronic |
| 0232 | Sor. 3. 16 | Cumin, pepper, absenthium, hyssop, butter and old olive oil bean sized and smeared with sweet oil or lily oil | v. sup. | Full ret. of mens. Flux chronic |
| 0233 | Sor. 3. 16 | White hellebore | oral | Full ret. of mens. Flux chronic |
| 0234 | Sor. 3. 16 | Long travel | rocking | Full ret. of mens. Flux chronic |
| 0235 | Sor. 3. 16 | Natural waters | bath | Full ret. of mens. Flux chronic |

| | | | | |
|---|---|---|---|---|
| 0236 | Sor. 3. 23 | Put in a warm light room and apply pressure to parts in pain | other, topical | Inflammation of uterus |
| 0237 | Sor. 3. 23 | Rubdown with ointment | bath | Inflammation of uterus |
| 0238 | Sor. 3. 23 | Venesection behind arm | venesection | Inflammation of uterus |
| 0239 | Sor. 3. 23 | Warm oil with water (Sitz bath) | bath | Inflammation of uterus |
| 0240 | Sor. 3. 23 | Fenugreek, linseed and mallow (Sitz bath) | bath | Inflammation of uterus |
| 0241 | Sor. 3. 23 | Fenugreek, linseed and mallow w/ egg mix | topical | Inflammation of uterus |
| 0242 | Sor. 3. 23 | Warm water as mouthwash and to drink | mouthwash, drink | Inflammation of uterus |
| 0243 | Sor. 3. 23 | Spelt gruel w/ honey water or water | diet | Inflammation of uterus |
| 0244 | Sor. 3. 23 | Gruel w/ honey | diet | Inflammation of uterus |
| 0245 | Sor. 3. 23 | Gruel w/ olive oil dill and salt | diet | Inflammation of uterus |
| 0246 | Sor. 3. 23 | Gruel w/ soaked bread | diet | Inflammation of uterus |
| 0247 | Sor. 3. 23 | Gruel w/ sipping eggs | diet | Inflammation of uterus |
| 0248 | Sor. 3. 23 | Give food only every second day | diet | Inflammation of uterus |
| 0249 | Sor. 3. 23 | Cupping dry followed by wet | cupping | Inflammation of uterus |
| 0250 | Sor. 3. 23 | Wet cupping of pubes and hypochondriac region | cupping | Inflammation of uterus |
| 0251 | Sor. 3. 23 | Use leeches if above ineffective | bleeding | Inflammation of uterus |
| 0252 | Sor. 3. 23 | Relaxing poultices bread w/ warm pork fat | poultices | Inflammation of uterus |
| 0253 | Sor. 3. 23 | Relaxing poultices bread boiled w/ wild marrow root | poultices | Inflammation of uterus |
| 0254 | Sor. 3. 23 | Relaxing poultices bread boiled w/ linseed w/ the finest meal | poultices | Inflammation of uterus |
| 0255 | Sor. 3. 23 | Relaxing poultices bread boiled w/ fenugreek | poultices | Inflammation of uterus |
| 0256 | Sor. 3. 23 | Relaxing poultices bread boiled with olive oil honey and a decoction of mallow or fenugreek | poultices | Inflammation of uterus |
| 0257 | Sor. 3. 23 | Warm oil anal injection (4 cyaths) | injection | Inflammation of uterus |
| 0258 | Sor. 3. 23 | Simple anal suppositories | suppository | Inflammation of uterus |
| 0259 | Sor. 3. 23 | Wool w/ warm olive oil | topical | Inflammation of uterus |

| | | | | |
|---|---|---|---|---|
| 0260 | Sor. 3. 23 | Juice of fenugreek, linseed or mallow beaten in oil and boiled with goose or chicken fat on wool | topical | Inflammation of uterus |
| 0261 | Sor. 3. 23 | 196 triturated with egg yolk by means of refined honey | topical | Inflammation of uterus |
| 0262 | Sor. 3. 28 | Place in warm bright room | other | Hysterical suffocation (seizure) (initial) |
| 0263 | Sor. 3. 28 | Straighten and bind all available limbs | other | Hysterical suffocation (seizure) (initial) |
| 0264 | Sor. 3. 28 | Move jaw and place warm compresses over the middle of her body | other, topical | To revive after a seizure |
| 0265 | Sor. 3. 28 | Warm all cool parts with body heat from hands | topical | Hysterical suffocation (seizure) (initial) |
| 0266 | Sor. 3. 28 | Dry cupping (groin and pubes) | cupping | Persistent aphonia |
| 0267 | Sor. 3. 28 | Cover with wool | topical | Hysterical suffocation (seizure) (initial) |
| 0268 | Sor. 3. 28 | Moisten groin with warm sweet oil | topical | Hysterical suffocation (seizure) (initial) |
| 0269 | Sor. 3. 28 | Put warm water in mouth, then honey water | mouthwash | Hysterical suffocation (seizure) (initial) |
| 0270 | Sor. 3. 28 | Movement in hammock | rocking | Hysterical suffocation (seizure) (initial) |
| 0271 | Sor. 3. 28 | Bleeding (if strength allows) | bleeding | Hysterical suffocation (seizure) (post initial) |
| 0272 | Sor. 3. 28 | Inject with warm olive oil, moisten parts, give warm water as mouthwash, abstain from food for 3 days | injection | Hysterical suffocation (seizure) (post initial) |
| 0273 | Sor. 3. 28 | Rub down and give gruel like food (every 2nd day till cured) | massage, diet | Hysterical suffocation (seizure) (3rd day) |
| 0274 | Sor. 3. 28 | Warm oil with water (Sitz bath) | bath | Hysterical suffocation (seizure) (3rd day) |
| 0275 | Sor. 3. 28 | Fenugreek, linseed and mallow (Sitz bath) | bath | Hysterical suffocation (seizure) (3rd day) |
| 0276 | Sor. 3. 28 | Fenugreek, linseed and mallow w/ egg mix | topical | Hysterical suffocation (seizure) (3rd day) |
| 0277 | Sor. 3. 28 | Linseed | topical | Hysterical suffocation (seizure) (3rd day) |
| 0278 | Sor. 3. 28 | Bread w/ warm hydromel | topical | Hysterical suffocation (seizure) (3rd day) |
| 0279 | Sor. 3. 28 | Fat, marrow, fenugreek, mallow, oil of lilies or henna oil | suppository | Hysterical suffocation (seizure) (3rd day) |
| 0280 | Sor. 3. 28 | Clyster of olive oil or oil w/ water | enema | Hysterical suffocation (seizure) (3rd day) |
| 0281 | Sor. 3. 28 | Wax salves and highly emollient suppositories | salve | Hysterical suffocation (seizure) (3rd day) |

| | | | | |
|---|---|---|---|---|
| 0282 | Sor. 3. 28 | Varied food, bath and wine | diet | Hysterical suffocation (seizure) (3rd day) |
| 0283 | Sor. 3. 28 | Passive exercises, promenades, vocal exercises, reading aloud, anointing, gymnastics baths and varied food | other | Hysterical suffocation (seizure) (chronic) (restorative) |
| 0284 | Sor. 3. 28 | Pungent diet | diet | Hysterical suffocation (seizure) (chronic) (active) |
| 0285 | Sor. 3. 28 | Pitch plaster | plaster | Hysterical suffocation (seizure) (chronic) (active) |
| 0286 | Sor. 3. 28 | Cupping | cupping | Hysterical suffocation (seizure) (chronic) (active) |
| 0287 | Sor. 3. 28 | Intense heat | other | Hysterical suffocation (seizure) (chronic) (active) |
| 0288 | Sor. 3. 28 | Vigorous local massage | massage | Hysterical suffocation (seizure) (chronic) (active) |
| 0289 | Sor. 3. 28 | Pungent sitz baths | bath | Hysterical suffocation (seizure) (chronic) (active) |
| 0290 | Sor. 3. 28 | Sprinkling powders | topical | Hysterical suffocation (seizure) (chronic) (active) |
| 0291 | Sor. 3. 28 | Irritating suppositories and poultices | suppository, poultice | Hysterical suffocation (seizure) (chronic) (active) |
| 0292 | Sor. 3. 28 | Mustard plasters | plaster | Hysterical suffocation (seizure) (chronic) (active) |
| 0293 | Sor. 3. 28 | Cyclic treatment | | Hysterical suffocation (seizure) (chronic) (active) |
| 0294 | Sor. 3. 28 | Choke by means of white hellebore | oral | Hysterical suffocation (seizure) (chronic) (active) |
| 0295 | Sor. 3. 28 | Provoke vomiting by radishes | oral | Hysterical suffocation (seizure) (chronic) (active) |
| 0296 | Sor. 3. 28 | Traveling by land and sea | other | Hysterical suffocation (seizure) (chronic) (active) |
| 0297 | Sor. 3. 28 | Natural waters | drink | Hysterical suffocation (seizure) (chronic) (active) |
| 0298 | Sor. 3. 29 | Lists of others treatments | | Hysterical suffocation (seizure) (chronic) (active) |
| 0299 | Sor. 3. 32 | Relaxing injections | injection | Air in uterus |
| 0300 | Sor. 3. 32 | Relaxing poultices | poultice | Air in uterus |
| 0301 | Sor. 3. 32 | Dry cupping | cupping | Air in uterus |
| 0302 | Sor. 3. 32 | Wet cupping | cupping | Air in uterus |
| 0303 | Sor. 3. 32 | Easy to digest foods | diet | Air in uterus |
| 0304 | Sor. 3. 32 | Midwife to remove the embedded clot (w/ finger) | other, surgery | Air in uterus |

| ID | Reference | Treatment | Type | Condition |
|---|---|---|---|---|
| 0305 | Sor. 3. 32 | Relaxing treatments | | Air in uterus (chronic) |
| 0306 | Sor. 3. 32 | Strengthen w/ warm ointments | ointment | Air in uterus (chronic)(remission) |
| 0307 | Sor. 3. 32 | Massage of the legs and effected parts | massage | Air in uterus (chronic)(remission) |
| 0308 | Sor. 3. 32 | Varied (pungent) food | diet | Air in uterus (chronic) |
| 0309 | Sor. 3. 32 | Pitch plaster on loins or abdomen | plaster | Air in uterus (chronic) |
| 0310 | Sor. 3. 32 | Sprinkle pitch plaster with natron or apply intense heat | plaster | Air in uterus (chronic) |
| 0311 | Sor. 3. 32 | Mustard and dried figs rubefacient (increases blood flow) | rubefacient | Air in uterus (chronic) |
| 0312 | Sor. 3. 32 | Barley w/ boiled figs, rue, Hyssop and honey | poultice | Air in uterus (chronic) |
| 0313 | Sor. 3. 32 | Natron, figs, absinthium | plaster | Air in uterus (chronic) |
| 0314 | Sor. 3. 32 | Ground grain w/ boiled figs, and hyssop | plaster | Air in uterus (chronic) |
| 0315 | Sor. 3. 32 | Seeds of cataplasm | plaster | Air in uterus (chronic) |
| 0316 | Sor. 3. 32 | Polyarchus | plaster | Air in uterus (chronic) |
| 0317 | Sor. 3. 32 | Bayberry (first with wax salve then alone) | bath | Air in uterus (chronic) |
| 0318 | Sor. 3. 32 | Carrots, Cretan daucus and pennyroyal w/ water | bath | Air in uterus (chronic) |
| 0319 | Sor. 3. 32 | Wormwood, hyssop, horehound, sweet bay or its fruits, cassia and spikenard | suppository | Air in uterus (chronic) |
| 0320 | Sor. 3. 32 | Rue, pennyroyal, honey, natron, and turpentine w/ galbanum, iris, rue, hyssop, and ox bile | suppository | Air in uterus (chronic) |
| 0321 | Sor. 3. 32 | Rich ground figs (1drachm), soft cyclamen root (2drachm), white aphronite (1 drachm) dip in milk | suppository | Air in uterus (chronic) |
| 0322 | Sor. 3. 32 | Cupping in circle wet and dry | cupping | Air in uterus (chronic) |
| 0323 | Sor. 3. 32 | Diospolis remedy | | Air in uterus (chronic) |
| 0324 | Sor. 3. 32 | Mint remedy | | Air in uterus (chronic) |
| 0325 | Sor. 3. 34 | Same as for air in uterus 299 -324 | | Soft swelling of uterus |
| 0326 | Sor. 3. 34 | Warm olive oil | v. sup. | Soft swelling of uterus |
| 0327 | Sor. 3. 34 | Henna or iris oil | v. sup. | Soft swelling of uterus |
| 0328 | Sor. 3. 38 | Warm poultices | poultice | The mole (exasperations) |

| | | | | |
|---|---|---|---|---|
| 0329 | Sor. 3. 38 | Cupping | cupping | The mole (exasperations) |
| 0330 | Sor. 3. 38 | Scarification | bleeding | The mole (exasperations) |
| 0331 | Sor. 3. 38 | Leeches | bleeding | The mole (exasperations) |
| 0332 | Sor. 3. 38 | Heat | other | The mole (exasperations) |
| 0333 | Sor. 3. 38 | Relaxing injections | injection | The mole (exasperations) |
| 0334 | Sor. 3. 38 | Softening suppository | suppository | The mole (exasperations) |
| 0335 | Sor. 3. 38 | Sitz baths | bath | The mole (exasperations) |
| 0336 | Sor. 3. 38 | Cerates boiled w/ marshmallow, and sweet olive or henna oil | | The mole (exasperations) |
| 0337 | Sor. 3. 38 | Diachylian cataplasm | poultice | The mole (exasperations) |
| 0338 | Sor. 3. 38 | Mnaseas cataplasm | poultice | The mole (exasperations) |
| 0339 | Sor. 3. 38 | Food of good juices which make good humours | diet | The mole (exasperations) |
| 0340 | Sor. 3. 38 | Bandage to alleviate downward pull | other | The mole (exasperations) |
| 0341 | Sor. 3. 38 | Restorative cures | | The mole (remissions) |
| 0342 | Sor. 3. 38 | Pitch plaster | plaster | The mole (remissions) |
| 0343 | Sor. 3. 38 | Application of heat | other | The mole (remissions) |
| 0344 | Sor. 3. 38 | Sun baths | bath | The mole (remissions) |
| 0345 | Sor. 3. 38 | Natron and salt massage | massage, bath | The mole (remissions) |
| 0346 | Sor. 3. 38 | Mustard and dried figs rubefacient (increases blood flow) | rubefacient | The mole (remissions) |
| 0347 | Sor. 3. 38 | Seeds of cataplasm | cataplasm | The mole (remissions) |
| 0348 | Sor. 3. 38 | Bayberry cataplasm | cataplasm | The mole (remissions) |
| 0349 | Sor. 3. 38 | Polyarchus | cataplasm | The mole (remissions) |
| 0350 | Sor. 3. 38 | Cephisophon | cataplasm | The mole (remissions) |
| 0351 | Sor. 3. 38 | Boiled sea water w/ sweet bay, bayberry, pennyroyal, hyssop, salvia, horehound, wormwood, dittany, centaury, germander, garlic germander | bath | The mole (remissions) |

| | | | |
|---|---|---|---|
| 0352 | Sor. 3. 38 | Butter, hyssop, goose fat, chicken fat, deer's marrow or brain, and honey or fig and raisin flesh w/ old olive oil or henna, iris, marjoram, amarakos, lilies or malabathron oil | bath | The mole (remissions) |
| 0353 | Sor. 3. 38 | Pungent diet | diet | The mole (remissions) |
| 0354 | Sor. 3. 38 | Cyclic treatment | | The mole (remissions) |
| 0355 | Sor. 3. 38 | Natural waters, shower baths, swimming in the sea or natural waters | bath | The mole (remissions) |
| 0356 | Sor. 3. 38 | Radishes for vomiting | oral | The mole (remissions) |
| 0357 | Sor. 3. 38 | Hellebore | oral | The mole (remissions) |
| 0358 | Sor. 3. 41 | Lie in small dark cool room | other | Uterine haemorrhage |
| 0359 | Sor. 3. 41 | Stay still cross legs | other | Uterine haemorrhage |
| 0360 | Sor. 3. 41 | Flat sponges soaked in cold water or vinegar applied to groin etc. And later the chest | topical compress | Uterine haemorrhage |
| 0361 | Sor. 3. 41 | Bandage limbs | other | Uterine haemorrhage |
| 0362 | Sor. 3. 41 | Cold water and fanning on face | bath, other | Uterine haemorrhage |
| 0363 | Sor. 3. 41 | Moisten head with fresh cold olive oil | bath | Uterine haemorrhage |
| 0364 | Sor. 3. 41 | Drink vinegar | drink | Uterine haemorrhage |
| 0365 | Sor. 3. 41 | Cold water | bath | Uterine haemorrhage |
| 0366 | Sor. 3. 41 | Vinegar | bath | Uterine haemorrhage |
| 0367 | Sor. 3. 41 | Myrtle berries | bath | Uterine haemorrhage |
| 0368 | Sor. 3. 41 | Dried roses | bath | Uterine haemorrhage |
| 0369 | Sor. 3. 41 | Omphakitis oak galls | bath | Uterine haemorrhage |
| 0370 | Sor. 3. 41 | Myrtle and lentils | bath | Uterine haemorrhage |
| 0371 | Sor. 3. 41 | Mastic | bath | Uterine haemorrhage |
| 0372 | Sor. 3. 41 | Pomegranate peels | bath | Uterine haemorrhage |
| 0373 | Sor. 3. 41 | Bramble blossom | bath | Uterine haemorrhage |

| | | | | |
|---|---|---|---|---|
| 0374 | Sor. 3. 41 | Oak leaves | bath | Uterine haemorrhage |
| 0375 | Sor. 3. 41 | Willow leaves | bath | Uterine haemorrhage |
| 0376 | Sor. 3. 41 | Tanning sumach | bath | Uterine haemorrhage |
| 0377 | Sor. 3. 41 | Juice of 367-376 | v. injection | Uterine haemorrhage |
| 0378 | Sor. 3. 41 | Juice of plantain, knotgrass, endive, black nightshade, fleawort, or perdikion | v. injection | Uterine haemorrhage |
| 0379 | Sor. 3. 41 | Hypocist and acacia juice w/ opium w/ vinegar | v. injection | Uterine haemorrhage |
| 0380 | Sor. 3. 41 | Omphakion (2 cyaths) | v. injection | Uterine haemorrhage |
| 0381 | Sor. 3. 41 | Juice of above with wool and inserted | v. sup. | Uterine haemorrhage |
| 0382 | Sor. 3. 41 | Sponge soaked in above be inserted | v. sup. | Uterine haemorrhage |
| 0383 | Sor. 3. 41 | Hot cupping loins groins and flanks | cupping | Uterine haemorrhage |
| 0384 | Sor. 3. 41 | Dates soaked in tart wine or vinegar w/ cerate of roses or quinces, ground leaves of myrtle or meddlers, or alum, aloe, blossoms of the wild vine, hypocist, acacia, omphakatis oak gall and freshly made olive oil or rose, myrtle, mastic, or quince oil | plaster | Uterine haemorrhage |
| 0385 | Sor. 3. 41 | Astringent cooling plaster: purslane w/ barley powder and vinegar or dates | plaster | Uterine haemorrhage |
| 0386 | Sor. 3. 41 | Astringent cooling plaster: henbane w/ barley powder and vinegar or dates | plaster | Uterine haemorrhage |
| 0387 | Sor. 3. 41 | Astringent cooling plaster: plantain w/ barley powder and vinegar or dates | plaster | Uterine haemorrhage |
| 0388 | Sor. 3. 41 | Astringent cooling plaster: fleawort w/ barley powder and vinegar or dates | plaster | Uterine haemorrhage |
| 0389 | Sor. 3. 41 | Astringent cooling plaster: black nightshade w/ barley powder and vinegar or dates | plaster | Uterine haemorrhage |
| 0390 | Sor. 3. 41 | Astringent cooling plaster: perdicion w/ barley powder and vinegar or dates | plaster | Uterine haemorrhage |
| 0391 | Sor. 3. 41 | Astringent cooling plaster: knotgrass w/ barley powder and vinegar or | plaster | Uterine haemorrhage |

| ID | Source | Recipe | Type | Condition |
|---|---|---|---|---|
| | | dates | | |
| 0392 | Sor. 3. 41 | Astringent cooling plaster: endive w/ barley powder and vinegar or dates | plaster | Uterine haemorrhage |
| 0393 | Sor. 3. 41 | Oak gall, pulverised frankincense, chalcites (equal) w/ sweet wine | v. sup. | Uterine haemorrhage |
| 0394 | Sor. 3. 41 | Ashes of sea sponge soaked in pitch | v. sup. | Uterine haemorrhage |
| 0395 | Sor. 3. 41 | Dry dregs of wine with astringent juices | v. sup. | Uterine haemorrhage |
| 0396 | Sor. 3. 41 | Black remedy (papyrus w/ vinegar or troches for dysentery) | oral | Uterine haemorrhage (w/ erosion) |
| 0397 | Sor. 3. 41 | Rice in cold water or vinegar, or spelt or bread and soft boiled egg in vinegar | diet | Uterine haemorrhage (after sponging face) |
| 0398 | Sor. 3. 41 | Endive or plantain in vinegar and freshly ground sumach | diet | Uterine haemorrhage (after sponging face) |
| 0399 | Sor. 3. 41 | Fresh olive oil well boiled | diet | Uterine haemorrhage (after sponging face) |
| 0400 | Sor. 3. 41 | Apples and baked quinces or boiled pears and a bit of ringdove breast meat boiled in vinegar and stuffed with myrtle berries | diet | Uterine haemorrhage (after sponging face) |
| 0401 | Sor. 3. 41 | partridge or francolin | diet | Uterine haemorrhage (after sponging face) |
| 0402 | Sor. 3. 41 | Some wine | diet | Uterine haemorrhage (after time of sympathetic reactions) |
| 0403 | Sor. 3. 41 | Bath when completely firm | bath | Uterine haemorrhage (after sponging face) (when firm) |
| 0404 | Sor. 3. 44 | Treat as for uterine haemorrhage if non painful or ulcerating | | Flux of the uterus (non-painful non-ulcerating) |
| 0405 | Sor. 3. 44 | Mild astringent potions: Lotus tree sawdust, w/ Samian earth, w/ 2 cyaths of water and tart wine together with rennet of hare, calf lamb or deer or grapestones, myrtle berries, pomegranate peel or pine bark (2 drachmas) | oral | Flux of the uterus (non- painful non ulcerating) |
| 0406 | Sor. 3. 44 | Theban dates, quinces and apples | oral | Flux of the uterus (non-painful non ulcerating) |
| 0407 | Sor. 3. 44 | Tragos, spelt or barley juice | injection | Flux of the uterus (painful) (non-ulcerating) |
| 0408 | Sor. 3. 44 | Warming poultices | poultice | Flux of the uterus (painful) (non-ulcerating) |
| 0409 | Sor. 3. 44 | Warm thin food | diet | Flux of the uterus (painful) (non-ulcerating) |
| 0410 | Sor. 3. 44 | Treat as for painful flux | other | Flux of the uterus (painful) (clean ulcerating) |

| | | | | |
|---|---|---|---|---|
| 0411 | Sor. 3. 44 | As for dysentery | other | Flux of the uterus (painful) (dirty ulcerating) |
| 0412 | Sor. 3. 44 | Passive exercises, promenades, vocal exercises, | other | Flux of the uterus (chronic) (remission) |
| 0413 | Sor. 3. 44 | The restorative cure, baths, wine in moderation, varied food, intense heat | other | Flux of the uterus (chronic) (remission) |
| 0414 | Sor. 3. 44 | Sun baths, metasyncretic cupping, pitch plasters, massage with hands or linen towel | other | Flux of the uterus (chronic) (remission) |
| 0415 | Sor. 3. 44 | Depilatories or metasyncretic unguents, mustard plasters | other | Flux of the uterus (chronic) (remission) |
| 0416 | Sor. 3. 44 | Radishes for vomiting, pungent diet, cyclic cure, swimming, shower baths in natural waters | other | Flux of the uterus (chronic) (remission) |
| 0417 | Sor. 3. 44 | Land or sea travel, sitz baths | bath | Flux of the uterus (chronic) (remission) |
| 0418 | Sor. 3. 44 | Irritating vaginal suppositories | v. sup. | Flux of the uterus (chronic) (remission) |
| 0419 | Sor. 3. 46 | Seat in decoctions of roses, myrtle, mastich, bramble | bath | Flux of semen |
| 0420 | Sor. 3. 46 | Acacia and hypocist in tart wine on lower abdomen and groins | massage | Flux of semen |
| 0421 | Sor. 3. 46 | Dates quinces and myrtle | poultice | Flux of semen |
| 0422 | Sor. 3. 46 | Vomit after meals or on empty stomach | oral | Flux of semen |
| 0423 | Sor. 3. 46 | Upper exercise and massage | other | Flux of semen |
| 0424 | Sor. 3. 46 | Halikakabon root dried (1 drachma) w/ water | oral | Flux of semen |
| 0425 | Sor. 3. 46 | Seed of the chaste tree w/ water | oral | Flux of semen |
| 0426 | Sor. 3. 46 | Seed of hemp or rue | oral | Flux of semen |
| 0427 | Sor. 3. 46 | Dry diet w/ roast foul and dry wine | diet | Flux of semen |
| 0428 | Sor. 3. 46 | Gymnastics and sweeting, massage cold baths anoint abdomen and loins in rose oil | other, massage | Flux of semen (chronic) |
| 0429 | Sor. 3. 48 | Treat as chronic lax disease | | Atony of the uterus |
| 0430 | Sor. 3. 48 | Sea sponges w/ diluted vinegar on pubes and loins | compress | Prevent miscarriage |
| 0431 | Sor. 3. 48 | Astringent sitz baths | bath | Atony of the uterus |
| 0432 | Sor. 3. 48 | Rose, narcissus, lily or quince oil injected into uterus | injection | Atony of the uterus |
| 0433 | Sor. 3. 48 | Exercise | other | Atony of the uterus |
| 0434 | Sor. 3. 48 | Little food mainly meat mildly astringent with astringent wine, no dairy | diet | Atony of the uterus |

| | | | | |
|---|---|---|---|---|
| 0435 | Sor. 4. 7 | Position them on their knees for delivery | other | Women fat or with concave loins |
| 0436 | Sor. 4. 7 | Warm sweet olive oil w/ decoction of fenugreek, mallow, linseed or egg whites | anointment | |
| 0437 | Sor. 4. 7 | Linseed or fenugreek in olive oil on loins pubes and abdomen | bath | |
| 0438 | Sor. 4. 7 | Oily sitz bath or fomentation applied with sponges and quickly removed with linen | compress | |
| 0439 | Sor. 4. 7 | Warm olive oil or grain bags | rocking | Pain |
| 0440 | Sor. 4. 7 | Move them about on a litter | other | |
| 0441 | Sor. 4. 7 | Breathing control | diet | |
| 0442 | Sor. 4. 7 | Weak women to be fed simple food in interval | ointment | |
| 0443 | Sor. 4. 7 | Push aside blockages of the uterus with ointment | surgery | |
| 0444 | Sor. 4. 7 | Remove blockages of the uterus surgically | enema | |
| 0445 | Sor. 4. 7 | Water w/ oil or hydromel | surgery | Retained faeces |
| 0446 | Sor. 4. 7 | Ureteral catheter | surgery | Retained urine |
| 0447 | Sor. 4. 8 | Move foetus | surgery | |
| 0448 | Sor. 4. 9 - 10 | Hook extraction | surgery | Failed to deliver correctly (save mother) |
| 0449 | Sor. 4. 11 | Amputate prolapsed limbs | surgery | Severe prolapse which cannot be straightened or death |
| 0450 | Sor. 4. 11 | Drain foetus of fluids to make it small and cause it to collapse | surgery | |
| 0451 | Sor. 4. 12 | Reassemble foetus to ensure no parts remain | surgery | |
| 0452 | Sor. 4. 16 | Follow umbilical to placenta and remove it by lateral movements | surgery | Retention of the placenta |
| 0453 | Sor. 4. 16 | Treat as an inflammation: injections poultice and warm foods | poultice, diet | Retention of the placenta w/ contracted cervix |
| 0454 | Sor. 4. 37 | Wash uterus with cold water or diluted vinegar and adjust with finger | topical | Uterine prolapse |
| 0455 | Sor. 4. 37 | Adjust with sponge | topical | Uterine prolapse |
| 0456 | Sor. 4. 37 | Apply sponge w/ diluted vinegar or wool to vagina and bind thighs | topical | Uterine prolapse |
| 0457 | Sor. 4. 37 | Fast for three days then give simple food every second day | diet | Uterine prolapse |
| 0458 | Sor. 4. 38 | Enema and catheter | enema | Retention of urine or faeces |

| | | | | |
|---|---|---|---|---|
| 0459 | Sor. 4. 38 | Bathe prolapsed part with lukewarm oil | bath | Uterine prolapse |
| 0460 | Sor. 4. 38 | Use a woollen tampon coated in thin linen w/ diluted vinegar, acacia juice or hypocist w/ wine increasing depth into vagina | topical | Uterine prolapse |
| 0461 | Sor. 4. 38 | Wool with astringent wine over vagina | compress | Uterine prolapse |
| 0462 | Sor. 4. 38 | Cover lower abdomen with sponges and diluted vinegar | compress | Uterine prolapse |
| 0463 | Sor. 4. 38 | Cover abdomen pubes and loins w/ sponges and diluted vinegar and bandage them | compress | Uterine prolapse |
| 0464 | Sor. 4. 38 | Cupping on each flank | cupping | Uterine prolapse |
| 0465 | Sor. 4. 38 | Sweet smells continually | smell | Uterine prolapse |
| 0466 | Sor. 4. 38 | Warm dark tart wine sitz bath | bath | Uterine prolapse |
| 0467 | Sor. 4. 38 | Bramble myrtle, mastich or pomegranate peel sitz | bath | Uterine prolapse |
| 0468 | Sor. 4. 38 | Dates barley, groats pomegranate peel and lentils w/ oxymel | poultice | Uterine prolapse |
| 0469 | Sor. 4. 38 | Warm oil, water and oil, fenugreek, linseed or mallow juice | bath | Uterine prolapse (long duration) (white) |
| 0470 | Sor. 4. 39 | Bleeding | venesection | Uterine prolapse (long duration) (white) |
| 0471 | Sor. 4. 39 | Wash w/ warm diluted vinegar, sitz bath in same | bath | Uterine prolapse (chronic) |
| 0472 | Sor. 4. 39 | Dry cupping | cupping | Uterine prolapse (chronic) |
| 0473 | Sor. 4. 39 | Dates or quince | plaster | Uterine prolapse (chronic) |
| 0474 | Sor. 4. 39 | Willow | plaster | Uterine prolapse (chronic) |
| 0475 | Sor. 4. 39 | Intense heat | other | Uterine prolapse (chronic)(metasyncretic) |
| 0476 | Sor. 4. 39 | Pungent unctions | anointment | |
| 0477 | Sor. 4. 39 | Mustard | plaster | |
| 0478 | Sor. 4. 39 | Natron, raisins and salt | v. sup. | |
| 0479 | Sor. 4. 39 | Treat as for ulceration | | Uterine prolapse (black) |
| 0480 | Sor. 4. 39 | Amputate black parts | surgery | Uterine prolapse (black) |
| 0481 | Plin. 20. 2 | Elaterium (juice of the seed of wild (exploding) cucumber) | lozenge | Dim vision |

| ID | Source | Preparation | Form | Ailment |
|---|---|---|---|---|
| 0482 | Plin. 20. 2 | Elaterium (juice of the seed of wild (exploding) cucumber) | lozenge | Eye diseases |
| 0483 | Plin. 20. 2 | Elaterium (juice of the seed of wild (exploding) cucumber) | lozenge | Sores of the eyes |
| 0484 | Plin. 20. 2 | Wild cucumber root boiled in vinegar | ointment | Gout |
| 0485 | Plin. 20. 2 | Wild cucumber root boiled in vinegar (juice) | ointment | Toothache |
| 0486 | Plin. 20. 2 | Wild cucumber elaterium dried w/ resin | ointment | Impetigo |
| 0487 | Plin. 20. 2 | Wild cucumber elaterium dried w/ resin | ointment | Itch |
| 0488 | Plin. 20. 2 | Wild cucumber elaterium dried w/ resin | ointment | Psora and lichen |
| 0489 | Plin. 20. 2 | Wild cucumber elaterium dried w/ resin | ointment | Parotid swellings |
| 0490 | Plin. 20. 2 | Wild cucumber elaterium dried w/ resin | ointment | Superficial abscesses |
| 0491 | Plin. 20. 2 | Wild cucumber elaterium dried w/ resin | ointment | Restores natural colour to scars |
| 0492 | Plin. 20. 2 | Juice of leaves of ecballium elaterium (squirting cucumber) w/ vinegar | ear drops | Deafness |
| 0493 | Plin. 20. 3 | Keep a cucumber fastened to her body without it touching the ground | other | Conception is aided |
| 0494 | Plin. 20. 3 | Seeds of cucumber wrapped in rams wool tied to her loins (and removed after delivery) | other | Labour |
| 0495 | Plin. 20. 3 | Seeds of the 'scorpion' cucumber or elaterium | purge or emetic | Scorpion sting |
| 0496 | Plin. 20. 3 | Seeds of the 'scorpion' cucumber or elaterium 1/2 to 1 obolus | purge or emetic | Purge |
| 0497 | Plin. 20. 3 | Seeds of the 'scorpion' cucumber or elaterium 1/2 to 1 obolus | drink | Phthiriasis or dropsy |
| 0498 | Plin. 20. 3 | Seeds of the 'scorpion' cucumber or elaterium w/ honey or old olive oil | oral? | Quinsy or tracheal afflictions |
| 0499 | Plin. 20. 4 | Serpentine/stray cucumber | decoction | Gout |
| 0500 | Plin. 20. 4 | Serpentine/stray cucumber | decoction | Diseases of the joints |
| 0501 | Plin. 20. 4 | Serpentine/stray cucumber seed dried in sun and pounded (20 Denarii) w/ water (1/2 sextus) | drink | Lumbago |
| 0502 | Plin. 20. 4 | Serpentine/stray cucumber w/ woman's milk | liniment | Sudden tumours |
| 0503 | Plin. 20. 4 | Elaterium | | Promotes lactation causes abortion |
| 0504 | Plin. 20. 4 | Elaterium (injected in nostrils) | injection | Asthma |
| 0505 | Plin. 20. 4 | Elaterium (injected in nostrils) | injection | Jaundice |

| | | | | |
|---|---|---|---|---|
| 0506 | Plin. 20. 4 | Elaterium (smeared on face) | ointment | Removes freckles and spots |
| 0507 | Plin. 20. 5 | Cultivated cucumber seed (three finger pinch) pounded w/ cumin w/ wine | drink | Coughs |
| 0508 | Plin. 20. 5 | Cultivated cucumber seed w/ woman's milk | drink | Phrenitis (malaria: raving and delirium) |
| 0509 | Plin. 20. 5 | Cultivated cucumber seed w/ acetabulum | topical | Dysentery |
| 0510 | Plin. 20. 5 | Cultivated cucumber seed w/ equal weight of cumin | topical | Excretion of pus |
| 0511 | Plin. 20. 5 | Cultivated cucumber seed w/ hydromel | drink | Diseases of the liver |
| 0512 | Plin. 20. 5 | Cultivated cucumber seed w/ sweet wine | drink | Diuretic |
| 0513 | Plin. 20. 5 | Cultivated cucumber seed w/ cumin | enema | Kidney pain |
| 0514 | Plin. 20. 6 | Pepones | oral | Laxative (constipation) |
| 0515 | Plin. 20. 6 | Pepones pulp | topical | Flux or pain of eyes |
| 0516 | Plin. 20. 6 | Pepones root | topical | Ceria (hard honey comb like sores) |
| 0517 | Plin. 20. 6 | Pepones root dried and ground into flower (4 oboli) with hydromel w/ half mile walk | drink | Emetic |
| 0518 | Plin. 20. 6 | Pepones root dried and ground into flower | topical | Skin smoothing cosmetics |
| 0519 | Plin. 20. 6 | Pepones rind | topical emetic | Clears face of spots |
| 0520 | Plin. 20. 6 | Gourd leaves topical application | topical emetic | Clears face of spots |
| 0521 | Plin. 20. 6 | Gourd leaves w/ honey | topical | Night rash |
| 0522 | Plin. 20. 6 | Gourd leaves w/ honey and wine | topical | Dog bites, multipede and 'seps' bites |
| 0523 | Plin. 20. 6 | Cucumber | smell | Revives those who have fainted |
| 0524 | Plin. 20. 7 | Σομφός chewed | oral | Good for stomach |
| 0525 | Plin. 20. 8 | Colocynthus dried drastic purge | oral | Purgative |
| 0526 | Plin. 20. 8 | Colocynthus enema | enema | Problems with the bowels, kidneys and loins |
| 0527 | Plin. 20. 8 | Colocynthus enema | enema | Paralysis |
| 0528 | Plin. 20. 8 | Colocynthus dry powder w/ boiled honey pills | oral | Stomach |
| 0529 | Plin. 20. 8 | Seven colocynthus seeds followed by hydromel | oral | Jaundice |

| | | | | |
|---|---|---|---|---|
| 0530 | Plin. 20. 8 | Colocynthus pulp w/ wormwood and salt | oral | Toothache |
| 0531 | Plin. 20. 8 | Colocynthus juice w/ warm vinegar | oral | Loose teeth firm |
| 0532 | Plin. 20. 8 | Colocynthus juice w/ oil | bath | Pains of spine, loins and hips |
| 0533 | Plin. 20. 8 | Colocynthus seeds in cloth on body | topical | Periodic fever |
| 0534 | Plin. 20. 8 | Colocynthus warmed juice | drops | Ear ache |
| 0535 | Plin. 20. 8 | Colocynthus inner pulp | topical | Corns and ἀποστήματα |
| 0536 | Plin. 20. 8 | Juice from boiling colocynthus pulp and seeds | | Loose teeth firm and stops toothache |
| 0537 | Plin. 20. 8 | Boiled colocynthus mixture w/ wine | | Inflammation of the eye |
| 0538 | Plin. 20. 8 | Colocynthus leaves w/ cypress leaves burned in a clay put w/ goose grease | topical | Cures wounds |
| 0539 | Plin. 20. 8 | Fresh colocynthus bark | | Cools gout and inflammations of the head (especially babies) |
| 0540 | Plin. 20. 8 | Fresh colocynthus bark or seeds | | Erysipelas (shingles) |
| 0541 | Plin. 20. 8 | Juice from scrapings w/ rose oil and vinegar (liniment) | liniment | Cools fever |
| 0542 | Plin. 20. 8 | Dust of the dry fruit | | Heals wounds |
| 0543 | Plin. 20. 8 | As food | oral | Stomach, ulcerations of the intestines and bladder |
| 0544 | Plin. 20. 9 | Hot turnip | | Chilblains prevents feet from becoming chilled |
| 0545 | Plin. 20. 9 | Hot decoction | oral | Cold gout |
| 0546 | Plin. 20. 9 | Raw pounded w/ salt | | All ailments of the feet |
| 0547 | Plin. 20. 9 | Turnip seed liniment or drunk with wine | liniment or drunk | Snake bites and poisons preventative |
| 0548 | Plin. 20. 9 | Turnip seed w/ wine and oil | drunk | Antidote to poisons |
| 0549 | Plin. 20. 9 | As food | oral | Aphrodisiac |
| 0550 | Plin. 20. 9 | As food w/ rocket | oral | Aphrodisiac more potent |
| 0551 | Plin. 20. 9 | Turnip roasted w/ grease | ointment | Pain with joints |
| 0552 | Plin. 20. 10 | Turnip seed w/ meal of vetches, barley wheat and lupines | topical | Smoothing the face/skin |
| 0553 | Plin. 20. 11 | Angular leaved navew decoction w/ hydromel or a drachma of the juice | drink | Purgings of women, the bladder and urine |

| | | | | |
|---|---|---|---|---|
| 0554 | Plin. 20. 11 | Angular leaved navew seed roasted and ground w/ warm water (4 cyathi) | drink | Dysentery |
| 0555 | Plin. 20. 11 | Angular leaved navew seed roasted and ground w/ warm water (4 cyaths) | drink | Prevents urination unless linseed drink is take with it |
| 0556 | Plin. 20. 11 | Bunias navew (like radish and turnip) | oral | Poisons antidote |
| 0557 | Plin. 20. 12 | Wiled radish | oral | Diuretic |
| 0558 | Plin. 20. 13 | Cultivated radishes | oral | Purge the stomach, loosen phlegm, promote urine and removes bile |
| 0559 | Plin. 20. 13 | Radish skin in wine in morning (too 3 cyathi) | drink | Break up and remove gall stones |
| 0560 | Plin. 20. 13 | Radish skin w/ vinegar and water | liniment | Snake bites |
| 0561 | Plin. 20. 13 | To eat on empty stomach in morning w/ honey | oral | Cough |
| 0562 | Plin. 20. 13 | Roasted radish seed | oral | Cough |
| 0563 | Plin. 20. 13 | Radish amulet | other | Phthiriasis |
| 0564 | Plin. 20. 13 | Decoction of leaves w/ water (2 cyathi) | drink | Phthiriasis |
| 0565 | Plin. 20. 13 | Neat radish juice (2 cyathi) | drink | Phthiriasis |
| 0566 | Plin. 20. 13 | Liniment of crushed radish | liniment | Inflammation |
| 0567 | Plin. 20. 13 | Radish skins w/ honey | liniment | Recent bruise |
| 0568 | Plin. 20. 13 | Eaten at their hottest | oral | Lethargic persons |
| 0569 | Plin. 20. 13 | Radish seed roasted beaten and mixed with honey | oral | Asthmatics |
| 0570 | Plin. 20. 13 | Radish or seed rubbed on hands | topical | Horned viper and scorpion antidote |
| 0571 | Plin. 20. 13 | Radish | | Fungi, henbane, and bulls blood antidote |
| 0572 | Plin. 20. 13 | Radish seeds w/ water | drink | Mistletoe poisoning |
| 0573 | Plin. 20. 13 | Radish juice | drink | Mistletoe poisoning |
| 0574 | Plin. 20. 13 | Radish w/ vinegar or mustard | oral | Dropsy, lethargies, epilepsy and melancholia |
| 0575 | Plin. 20. 13 | Radish | oral | Iliac (disease of the bowels) |
| 0576 | Plin. 20. 13 | Radish | oral | Coeliac |
| 0577 | Plin. 20. 13 | Radish with honey | oral | Ulcers of the intestines and chest suppurations |

| ID | Source | Description | Route | Use |
|---|---|---|---|---|
| 0578 | Plin. 20. 13 | Radish with honey cooked in mud | oral | Promotes menstrual discharge |
| 0579 | Plin. 20. 13 | Radish with vinegar or honey | oral | Intestinal worms |
| 0580 | Plin. 20. 13 | Radish boiled to a third w/ wine | oral decoction | Intestinal hernia |
| 0581 | Plin. 20. 13 | Radish cooked | oral | Spitting blood |
| 0582 | Plin. 20. 13 | Radish feed cooked to women lying | oral | Increase lactation |
| 0583 | Plin. 20. 13 | Radish rubbed on a woman's head when hair falls out | topical | Hair falls out |
| 0584 | Plin. 20. 13 | Radish placed on navel for pains of the womb | topical | Pain in womb |
| 0585 | Plin. 20. 13 | Radish return scars to normal colour | topical | Scaring |
| 0586 | Plin. 20. 13 | Radish seed in water | decoction | Phagedaenae ulcers |
| 0587 | Plin. 20. 13 | Radish as food | oral | Aphrodisiac (damages voice) |
| 0588 | Plin. 20. 13 | Leaves of long radish | oral | Improve sight |
| 0589 | Plin. 20. 13 | Hyssop | oral | Radish overdose |
| 0590 | Plin. 20. 13 | Radish juice in ear | ear drops | Deafness |
| 0591 | Plin. 20. 13 | Eaten after a meal | oral | To prevent vomiting |
| 0592 | Plin. 20. 14 | Marsh mallow | | Ulcers, broken cartilages and bones |
| 0593 | Plin. 20. 14 | Marshmallow leaves in water | drink | Relax the bowels |
| 0594 | Plin. 20. 14 | Marsh mallow | liniment | Bee, wasp, and hornet stings |
| 0595 | Plin. 20. 14 | Marshmallow roots, dug up before dawn and wrapped in natural wool of a sheep which has given birth to a ewe. Bound on scrofulous sores. (possibly dug up with gold tool) | topical | Scrofulous sores |
| 0596 | Plin. 20. 14 | Marshmallow root w/ wine | liniment | Gout without swelling |
| 0597 | Plin. 20. 15 | Staphylinus seed crushed w/wine | drink | Swollen belly |
| 0598 | Plin. 20. 15 | Staphylinus seed crushed w/wine | drink | Hysterical suffocation and pains of women |
| 0599 | Plin. 20. 15 | Staphylinus seed crushed w/bread and raisin wine | drink | Belly-ache |
| 0600 | Plin. 20. 15 | Staphylinus | | Diuretic |

| | | | | |
|---|---|---|---|---|
| 0601 | Plin. 20. 15 | Fresh staphylinus w/ honey | oral | Treats phagedaenic ulcers |
| 0602 | Plin. 20. 15 | Staphylinus dry sprinkled on flower | oral | Treats phagedaenic ulcers |
| 0603 | Plin. 20. 15 | Staphylinus root w/ hydromel | oral | Liver, spleen loins and kidney afflictions |
| 0604 | Plin. 20. 15 | Staphylinus root w/ hydromel | oral | Chronic dysentery |
| 0605 | Plin. 20. 15 | Staphylinus root (4 oz.) Boiled in milk | drink | Strangury |
| 0606 | Plin. 20. 15 | Staphylinus root (4 oz.) w/ water | drink | Dropsy |
| 0607 | Plin. 20. 15 | Staphylinus root (4 oz.) w/ water | drink | Opisthotonic (tetanus), tetanus, pleurisy and epilepsy |
| 0608 | Plin. 20. 15 | As food | oral | Suffer no harm when bitten by a snake |
| 0609 | Plin. 20. 15 | Staphylinus w/ axle grease | ointment | Bites |
| 0610 | Plin. 20. 15 | Staphylinus leaves chewed | oral (mastication) | Indigestion |
| 0611 | Plin. 20. 15 | Staphylinus eaten | oral | Aphrodisiac |
| 0612 | Plin. 20. 15 | Cultivated staphylinus seed w/ wine vinegar and water. | drink | Scorpion sting |
| 0613 | Plin. 20. 15 | Staphylinus root | dentifrice | Toothache |
| 0614 | Plin. 20. 16 | Gingidion cooked or raw | oral | Stomach |
| 0615 | Plin. 20. 17 | Wild parsnip w/ vinegar and silphium | oral | Stimulates appetite |
| 0616 | Plin. 20. 17 | Wild parsnip w/ pepper and honey wine | oral | Stimulates appetite |
| 0617 | Plin. 20. 17 | Wild parsnip w/ fish sauce | oral | Stimulates appetite |
| 0618 | Plin. 20. 17 | Wild parsnip | oral | Diuretic |
| 0619 | Plin. 20. 17 | Wild parsnip | oral | Aphrodisiac |
| 0620 | Plin. 20. 17 | Wild parsnip | drink | A cordial in convalescence |
| 0621 | Plin. 20. 17 | Wild parsnip | drink | Useful after lots of vomiting |
| 0622 | Plin. 20. 17 | Wild parsnip | oral | Mercury poisoning |
| 0623 | Plin. 20. 17 | Wild parsnip | oral | Occasional incontinence |
| 0624 | Plin. 20. 17 | Wild parsnip juice w/ goats milk | drink | Looseness of the bowels |

| ID | Reference | Preparation | Method | Use |
|---|---|---|---|---|
| 0625 | Plin. 20. 18 | Heartwort seed w/ white wine | drink | Chronic cough, ruptures, and convulsions |
| 0626 | Plin. 20. 18 | Heartwort seed (2-3 spoonful's) w/ white wine | drink | Opisthotonic (tetanus), liver problems, colic and strangury |
| 0627 | Plin. 20. 18 | Heartwort leaves | oral | Aid parturition |
| 0628 | Plin. 20. 18 | Heartwort leaves | topical | Erysipelas (shingles) |
| 0629 | Plin. 20. 18 | Heartwort leaves or seed | oral | Aids digestion |
| 0630 | Plin. 20. 18 | Heartwort | oral, drink and injection | Veterinary uses |
| 0631 | Plin. 20. 19 | Elecampain (while fasting) | masticant | Strengthens the teeth |
| 0632 | Plin. 20. 19 | Elecampain removed from the ground without touching it (confection) | confection | Cough |
| 0633 | Plin. 20. 19 | Juice of boiled elecampain root | drink | Expels worms |
| 0634 | Plin. 20. 19 | Dry powdered elecampain root | oral | Cough, convulsions, flatulence, and afflictions of the trachea |
| 0635 | Plin. 20. 19 | Elecampain | oral | Keeps off bite of poisonous creatures |
| 0636 | Plin. 20. 19 | Elecampain leaves steeped in wine | drink | Lumbago |
| 0637 | Plin. 20. 20 | Onions | smell | Feebleness of vision |
| 0638 | Plin. 20. 20 | Onion juice in eye | topical | Feebleness of vision |
| 0639 | Plin. 20. 20 | Onions | oral | Induce sleep |
| 0640 | Plin. 20. 20 | Onions w/ bread | masticant | Heal sores of the mouth |
| 0641 | Plin. 20. 20 | Fresh onions w/ vinegar | topical bandage | Dog bites and abrasions |
| 0642 | Plin. 20. 20 | Dry onions w/ honey and wine | topical bandage | Dog bites and abrasions |
| 0643 | Plin. 20. 20 | Onions cooked in ash w/ barley flour | topical | Fluxes of the eyes |
| 0644 | Plin. 20. 20 | Onions cooked in ash w/ barley flour | topical | Sores of the genitals |
| 0645 | Plin. 20. 20 | Onion juice | ointment | Eye sores |
| 0646 | Plin. 20. 20 | Onion juice | ointment | Albugo (eye disease of unusual whiteness) |

| | | | | |
|---|---|---|---|---|
| 0647 | Plin. 20. 20 | Onion juice | ointment | Argema (eye disease w/ white speck on black of eye) |
| 0648 | Plin. 20. 20 | Onion juice w/ honey | ointment | Snake bites |
| 0649 | Plin. 20. 20 | Onion juice w/ honey | ointment | Ulcers |
| 0650 | Plin. 20. 20 | Onion juice w/ woman's milk w/ goose grease or honey | ear drops | Sore ear laps, singing, hardness of hearing |
| 0651 | Plin. 20. 20 | Onion juice w/ water | drink | Sudden dumbness |
| 0652 | Plin. 20. 20 | Onion juice | gargle | Toothache |
| 0653 | Plin. 20. 20 | Onion juice | topical | Animal bites especially scorpions |
| 0654 | Plin. 20. 20 | Crushed onions | liniment | Mange or itch |
| 0655 | Plin. 20. 20 | Boiled onions | oral | Dysentery or lumbago |
| 0656 | Plin. 20. 20 | Onion peelings burnet to ash w/ vinegar | topical | Snake bites |
| 0657 | Plin. 20. 20 | Onions in vinegar | topical | Multipede bites |
| 0658 | Plin. 20. 20 | Onions as food | oral | Healthy complexion |
| 0659 | Plin. 20. 20 | Onions eaten daily on an empty stomach | oral | Good health, good for stomach, loosen the bowels |
| 0660 | Plin. 20. 20 | Onions as suppository | suppository | Haemorrhoids |
| 0661 | Plin. 20. 20 | Onion juice w/ fennel juice | drink | Incipient dropsy |
| 0662 | Plin. 20. 20 | Onion juice w/ rue and honey | drink | Quinsy and lethargies |
| 0663 | Plin. 20. 21 | Leeks crushed w/ gall nut or mint (in nose) | nasal plugs | Nose bleeding |
| 0664 | Plin. 20. 21 | Leek juice w/ woman's milk | drink | Flux after miscarriage |
| 0665 | Plin. 20. 21 | Leek | | Chronic cough, and afflictions of the chest and lungs |
| 0666 | Plin. 20. 21 | Leek leaves | topical | Pimples, burns and epinyctis (perpetually running sore in corner of eye) |
| 0667 | Plin. 20. 21 | Pounded leeks w/ honey | | Other sores |
| 0668 | Plin. 20. 21 | Leaks in vinegar | topical | Bites of serpents, poisonous creatures and beasts |
| 0669 | Plin. 20. 21 | Leaks and goats gall | topical | Ear problems |

| | | | | |
|---|---|---|---|---|
| 0670 | Plin. 20. 21 | Leak w/ mead | ear drops | Ear problems |
| 0671 | Plin. 20. 21 | Leek w/ woman's milk | ear drops | Singing in ears |
| 0672 | Plin. 20. 21 | Leek juice in nostrils | nose drops | Headache |
| 0673 | Plin. 20. 21 | Leek juice (2 tablespoons) w/ honey (1 tablespoon) | ear drops | Headache at night |
| 0674 | Plin. 20. 21 | Leek juice w/ neat wine | drink | Scorpion and snake bite |
| 0675 | Plin. 20. 21 | Leek juice w/ 1/2 sextarius of wine | drink | Lumbago |
| 0676 | Plin. 20. 21 | Leek juice or leek as food | oral | Spitting blood, consumption, and chronic catarrhs |
| 0677 | Plin. 20. 21 | Juice (acetabulum) w/ barley water | drink | Jaundice, dropsy and kidney pains |
| 0678 | Plin. 20. 21 | Juice (acetabulum) w/ honey | drink | Purges womb |
| 0679 | Plin. 20. 21 | Leek | oral | Fugal poisons |
| 0680 | Plin. 20. 21 | Leek | oral | Applied to wounds |
| 0681 | Plin. 20. 21 | Leek | oral | Aphrodisiac |
| 0682 | Plin. 20. 21 | Leek | oral | Quenches thirst |
| 0683 | Plin. 20. 21 | Leek | oral | Pick me up after drinking |
| 0684 | Plin. 20. 21 | Leek | oral | Make voice brilliant |
| 0685 | Plin. 20. 22 | Headed leek juice w/ gall nut, frankincense or acacia gum | oral | Spitting blood |
| 0686 | Plin. 20. 22 | Headed leek juice | drink | Open constricted womb |
| 0687 | Plin. 20. 22 | Headed leek as food | oral | Increased female fertility |
| 0688 | Plin. 20. 22 | Headed leek beaten w/ honey | topical | Cleanses sores |
| 0689 | Plin. 20. 22 | Leek w/ barley water or eaten raw except head without bread only on alternating days | oral | Cough, catarrh of the chest, affections of lungs and trachea |
| 0690 | Plin. 20. 22 | Leek w/ barley water or eaten raw except head without bread only on alternating days | oral | Benefits voice, venery and sleep |
| 0691 | Plin. 20. 22 | The heads boiled in water (changed twice) | oral | Diarrhoea and chronic fluxes |
| 0692 | Plin. 20. 22 | Head leak skin decoction | topical | Dye for grey hair |
| 0693 | Plin. 20. 23 | Garlic | topical | Deters serpents and scorpions with its smell |

| | | | | |
|---|---|---|---|---|
| 0694 | Plin. 20. 23 | Garlic (drunk eaten or applied as ointment) | oral drink | Cures bites |
| 0695 | Plin. 20. 23 | Garlic w/ wine and brought up by vomiting | topical | Haemorrhoids (snake species) |
| 0696 | Plin. 20. 23 | Garlic | drink | Shrew mouse bite |
| 0697 | Plin. 20. 23 | Garlic | drink | Antidote for aconite (panther strangler) hen bane |
| 0698 | Plin. 20. 23 | Garlic w/ honey | ointment | Dog bites |
| 0699 | Plin. 20. 23 | Garlic (roasted in its own leaves) w/ oil | liniment | Serpent bites |
| 0700 | Plin. 20. 23 | Garlic (roasted in its own leaves) w/ oil | liniment | Bruises (including blisters) |
| 0701 | Plin. 20. 23 | Garlic fumigations | fumigation | Bring away placenta |
| 0702 | Plin. 20. 23 | Garlic ash w/ oil | topical | Running sores on head |
| 0703 | Plin. 20. 23 | Garlic cooked | oral | Asthmatics |
| 0704 | Plin. 20. 23 | Garlic w/ centaury | oral | Dropsy |
| 0705 | Plin. 20. 23 | Garlic in split fig | oral | Purge |
| 0706 | Plin. 20. 23 | Fresh garlic in neat wine w/ coriander | drink | Purge |
| 0707 | Plin. 20. 23 | Pounded garlic w/ milk | drink | Asthmatics |
| 0708 | Plin. 20. 23 | Garlic w/ wine | drink | Jaundice |
| 0709 | Plin. 20. 23 | Garlic w/ oil and pottage | | Iliac passion (severe colic) |
| 0710 | Plin. 20. 23 | Garlic w/ oil and pottage | liniment | Scrofulous sores |
| 0711 | Plin. 20. 23 | Raw garlic | oral | Mad men |
| 0712 | Plin. 20. 23 | Well boiled garlic | oral | Phrenitis (malaria: raving and delirium) |
| 0713 | Plin. 20. 23 | Pounded w/ vinegar and water | gargle | Quinsy |
| 0714 | Plin. 20. 23 | 3 ponded garlic heads w/ vinegar | gargle | Toothache |
| 0715 | Plin. 20. 23 | Garlic inserted into hollow teeth | topical | Toothache |
| 0716 | Plin. 20. 23 | Garlic juice w/ goose fat | ear drops | |
| 0717 | Plin. 20. 23 | Garlic w/ drink | drink | Phthiriasis and scurf |
| 0718 | Plin. 20. 23 | Garlic w/ vinegar and soda | injection | Phthiriasis and scurf |

| | | | | |
|---|---|---|---|---|
| 0719 | Plin. 20. 23 | Garlic boiled w/ milk | oral | Catarrhs |
| 0720 | Plin. 20. 23 | Garlic crushed and mixed w/ soft cheese | oral | Catarrhs |
| 0721 | Plin. 20. 23 | Garlic crushed and mixed w/ soft cheese | oral | Relieves hoarseness |
| 0722 | Plin. 20. 23 | Garlic in gruel of peas or beans | oral | Relieves hoarseness |
| 0723 | Plin. 20. 23 | Garlic boiled | oral | Benefits the voice |
| 0724 | Plin. 20. 23 | Garlic cooked in oxymel | oral | Expels tape worms and other intestinal parasites |
| 0725 | Plin. 20. 23 | Garlic in pottage | oral | Tenesmus |
| 0726 | Plin. 20. 23 | Well boiled garlic | ointment | Pains in the temples |
| 0727 | Plin. 20. 23 | Garlic cooked and beaten | ointment | Blisters |
| 0728 | Plin. 20. 23 | Garlic decoction w/ stale grease or milk | drink | Cough |
| 0729 | Plin. 20. 23 | Garlic roasted under live ashes and taken w/ equal amount of honey | oral | Cough and spitting blood or pus |
| 0730 | Plin. 20. 23 | Garlic w/ salt and oil | | Sprains and ruptures |
| 0731 | Plin. 20. 23 | Garlic w/ fat | oral | Tumours |
| 0732 | Plin. 20. 23 | Garlic w/ sulphur and resin | poultice | Draws pus from fistulas |
| 0733 | Plin. 20. 23 | Garlic w/ pitch | poultice | Extracts arrows |
| 0734 | Plin. 20. 23 | Garlic w/ wild marjoram | topical | Leprous sores, lichen and freckly eruptions (cleansed and cured) |
| 0735 | Plin. 20. 23 | Garlic ash w/ oil and fish sauce | liniment | Leprous sores, lichen and freckly eruptions (cleansed and cured) |
| 0736 | Plin. 20. 23 | Garlic ash w/ oil and fish sauce | liniment | Erysipelas (shingles) |
| 0737 | Plin. 20. 23 | Garlic ash and honey | topical | Returns normal colour to discoloured skin |
| 0738 | Plin. 20. 23 | Garlic as food or drink | oral | Epilepsy |
| 0739 | Plin. 20. 23 | One garlic head w/ dry wine and silphium (1 obolus) | drink | Quartan ague |
| 0740 | Plin. 20. 23 | Garlic boiled in broken beans and eaten | oral | Cough and suppuration of the chest |
| 0741 | Plin. 20. 23 | Garlic | oral | Induce sleep |
| 0742 | Plin. 20. 23 | Garlic w/ fresh coriander in neat wine | drink | Aphrodisiac |

| | | | | |
|---|---|---|---|---|
| 0743 | Plin. 20. 23 | Garlic drawbacks | | Dulls sight, creates flatulence, injures stomach, creates thirst |
| 0744 | Plin. 20. 23 | Garlic oral and topical | | Veterinary uses |
| 0745 | Plin. 20. 24 | Goat-lettuce juice thickened w /vinegar (2 obolii) and water (1 cyath) | drink | Dropsy |
| 0746 | Plin. 20. 24 | Goat-lettuce stalks and leaves crushed w/ salt | topical | Cut sinew |
| 0747 | Plin. 20. 24 | Pounded plant w/ vinegar (twice a month) | mouthwash | Toothache (preventative) |
| 0748 | Plin. 20. 25 | Caesapon lettuce pounded w/ pearl barley | ointment | Sores |
| 0749 | Plin. 20. 25 | ἰσάτις lettuce leaves pounded w/ pearl barley | ointment | Wounds |
| 0750 | Plin. 20. 25 | Lettuce used by wool dyers like sorrel roots or leaves | topical | Stops bleeding, heals phagedaenic or putrefying ulcers |
| 0751 | Plin. 20. 25 | Lettuce used by wool dyers like sorrel roots or leaves | topical | Spreading ulcers, tumours before suppuration and erysipelas |
| 0752 | Plin. 20. 25 | Lettuce used by wool dyers like sorrel roots or leaves in drink | drink | Good for spleen |
| 0753 | Plin. 20. 26 | Wild lettuce 'resin' (dry sap) w/ woman's milk | drink | Eye diseases, |
| 0754 | Plin. 20. 26 | Wild lettuce 'resin' (dry sap) w/ woman's milk | drink | White ulcers |
| 0755 | Plin. 20. 26 | Wild lettuce 'resin' (dry sap) w/ woman's milk | drink | Films |
| 0756 | Plin. 20. 26 | Wild lettuce 'resin' (dry sap) w/ woman's milk | drink | Wounds and inflammations |
| 0757 | Plin. 20. 26 | Wild lettuce 'resin' (dry sap) w/ woman's milk | drink | Dimness of sight |
| 0758 | Plin. 20. 26 | Wild lettuce 'resin' (dry sap) w/ woman's milk on wool | topical | Eye fluxes |
| 0759 | Plin. 20. 26 | Wild lettuce juice (less than 2 obolii) in vinegar and water | drink | Purges the bowels |
| 0760 | Plin. 20. 26 | Wild lettuce juice in wine | drink | Heals snake bites |
| 0761 | Plin. 20. 26 | Wiled lettuce leaves and stalks pounded w/ vinegar | drink | Heals snake bites |
| 0762 | Plin. 20. 26 | Wild lettuce leaves and stalks | ointment | Scorpion sting |
| 0763 | Plin. 20. 26 | Wild lettuce leaves and stalks w/ wine and vinegar | ointment | Poisonous spiders |
| 0764 | Plin. 20. 26 | Wiled lettuce | oral | Neutralises other poisons |
| 0765 | Plin. 20. 26 | Wiled lettuce w/ honey and vinegar | topical | Bowel troubles |
| 0766 | Plin. 20. 26 | Wild lettuce juice | drink | Difficulty making urine |

| | | | | |
|---|---|---|---|---|
| 0767 | Plin. 20. 26 | Wild lettuce juice (2 oboli) w/ vinegar and wine (1 cyathus) | drink | Dropsy |
| 0768 | Plin. 20. 26 | Lettuces | oral | Causes sleep |
| 0769 | Plin. 20. 26 | Lettuces | oral | Reduces sexual desires |
| 0770 | Plin. 20. 26 | Lettuces | oral | Cooling a heated body |
| 0771 | Plin. 20. 26 | Lettuces | oral | Cleansing the stomach |
| 0772 | Plin. 20. 26 | Lettuces | oral | Making blood |
| 0773 | Plin. 20. 26 | Lettuces | oral | Clams flatulence and belching |
| 0774 | Plin. 20. 26 | Lettuces | oral | Aids digestion |
| 0775 | Plin. 20. 26 | Lettuces | oral | Moderates eating |
| 0776 | Plin. 20. 26 | Lettuces | oral | Loosens thick phlegm |
| 0777 | Plin. 20. 26 | Lettuces | oral | Good for upset stomachs |
| 0778 | Plin. 20. 26 | Lettuce w/ oboli of digestive w/ sweet wine w/ squill or wormwood wine (if phlegm thick) | drink | Good for upset stomachs (w/ phlegm) |
| 0779 | Plin. 20. 26 | Lettuce w/ oboli of digestive w/ sweet wine w/ hyssop wine (If also has cough) | drink | Good for upset stomachs (w/ cough) |
| 0780 | Plin. 20. 26 | Lettuces w/ wild endive | oral | Colic affections and hardness in the abdomen |
| 0781 | Plin. 20. 26 | White lettuce (lots) | oral | Melancholic patients and bladder troubles |
| 0782 | Plin. 20. 26 | White lettuce w/ salt | oral | Burns (prior to blistering) |
| 0783 | Plin. 20. 26 | Lettuce w/ saltpetre then in wine | oral | Prevents the spread of ulcers |
| 0784 | Plin. 20. 26 | Lettuce pounded | topical | Erysipelas (shingles) |
| 0785 | Plin. 20. 26 | Lettuce stalks pounded w/ pearl barley and cold water | topical | Soothe cramps, sprains |
| 0786 | Plin. 20. 26 | Lettuce stalks pounded w/ pearl barley cold water and wine | topical | Eruptions of pimples |
| 0787 | Plin. 20. 26 | Bitter lettuce cooked | oral | Cholera |
| 0788 | Plin. 20. 26 | Lettuce juice | injection | Cholera |
| 0789 | Plin. 20. 26 | Lettuce stalks boiled | oral | Good for the stomach |
| 0790 | Plin. 20. 26 | Lettuce stalks boiled | oral | Good for sleep |

| | | | | |
|---|---|---|---|---|
| 0791 | Plin. 20. 26 | Milky bitter lettuce w /woman's milk | drink | Clarity of vision w/ bathing |
| 0792 | Plin. 20. 26 | Milky bitter lettuce w /woman's milk | drink | Eye troubles caused by chill |
| 0793 | Plin. 20. 26 | Lettuce w/ attic honey | oral | Chest complaints |
| 0794 | Plin. 20. 26 | Lettuce (food) | oral | Menstruation is regulated |
| 0795 | Plin. 20. 26 | Seed of cultivated lettuce | topical | Scorpion stings |
| 0796 | Plin. 20. 26 | Crushed lettuce seed w/ wine | drink | Prevent amorous dreams |
| 0797 | Plin. 20. 26 | Lettuce (food) | oral | Not harmed by noxious waters |
| 0798 | Plin. 20. 26 | Taken to often | | Impair eyesight |
| 0799 | Plin. 20. 27 | Beet roots soaked and hung out to dry | | Snakebites |
| 0800 | Plin. 20. 27 | White beet boiled w/ raw garlic | oral | Tapeworms |
| 0801 | Plin. 20. 27 | Dark roots boiled | oral | Remove dandruff |
| 0802 | Plin. 20. 27 | Dark beet juice | drink | Headache, giddiness, |
| 0803 | Plin. 20. 27 | Dark beet juice | ear drops | Noises in the ear |
| 0804 | Plin. 20. 27 | Dark beet juice | drink | Diuretic |
| 0805 | Plin. 20. 27 | Dark beet juice | injected | Dysentery and jaundice |
| 0806 | Plin. 20. 27 | Dark beet juice | liniment | Toothache and serpent bite |
| 0807 | Plin. 20. 27 | Beet | decoction | Chilblains |
| 0808 | Plin. 20. 27 | White beet on forehead | topical | Eye fluxes |
| 0809 | Plin. 20. 27 | White beet w/ alum | topical | Erysipelas (shingles) |
| 0810 | Plin. 20. 27 | White beet crushed | topical | Burns |
| 0811 | Plin. 20. 27 | White beet | topical | Eruptions of pimples |
| 0812 | Plin. 20. 27 | White beet boiled | topical | Spreading sores |
| 0813 | Plin. 20. 27 | White beet (raw) | topical | Mange and running sores on the head |
| 0814 | Plin. 20. 27 | White beet juice w/honey | nasal drops | Clears the head |
| 0815 | Plin. 20. 27 | White beet gently boiled w/ lentils and vinegar | oral | Relax the bowels |
| 0816 | Plin. 20. 27 | Beet boiled vigorously | oral | Prevents flux of stomach and bowels |

| | | | | |
|---|---|---|---|---|
| 0817 | Plin. 20. 28 | Wild beet leaves | topical | Good for burns |
| 0818 | Plin. 20. 28 | Wild beet seeds (1 acetabulum) | oral | Dysentery |
| 0819 | Plin. 20. 29 | Endive juice w/ rose oil and vinegar | drink | Headache |
| 0820 | Plin. 20. 29 | Endive oil w/ wine | drink | Pains of the liver and bladder |
| 0821 | Plin. 20. 29 | Endive oil | topical | Fluxes of the eyes |
| 0822 | Plin. 20. 30 | Chicory (food) | oral | Cool gatherings |
| 0823 | Plin. 20. 30 | Chicory | liniment | Cool gatherings |
| 0824 | Plin. 20. 30 | Boiled chicory juice | drink | Loosens bowels |
| 0825 | Plin. 20. 30 | Boiled chicory juice | drink | Benefits liver kidneys and stomach |
| 0826 | Plin. 20. 30 | Chicory boiled in vinegar | oral | Stops painful urination |
| 0827 | Plin. 20. 30 | Chicory boiled in vinegar w/ honey wine | drink | Jaundice (w/ no fever) |
| 0828 | Plin. 20. 30 | Chicory | oral? | Helps bladder |
| 0829 | Plin. 20. 30 | Chicory boiled down in water | oral | Purges women aids in dispelling dead foetus |
| 0830 | Plin. 20. 30 | Magi say: anoint w/ juice of the entire chicory plant w/ oil | bath | Become more popular and attain requests more easily |
| 0831 | Plin. 20. 31 | Wild chicory boiled | oral | Is astringent on a relaxed stomach |
| 0832 | Plin. 20. 31 | Wild chicory raw | oral | Tightens loose bowels |
| 0833 | Plin. 20. 31 | Wild chicory w/ lentils | oral | Dysentery |
| 0834 | Plin. 20. 31 | Wild and cultivated chicory | | Ruptures and cramps |
| 0835 | Plin. 20. 31 | Wild and cultivated chicory | | Flux of sperm |
| 0836 | Plin. 20. 32 | Seris (endive) | oral | Stomach (esp. Troubled by humours) |
| 0837 | Plin. 20. 32 | Seris w/ vinegar | oral | Cooling |
| 0838 | Plin. 20. 32 | Seris | liniment | Cooling |
| 0839 | Plin. 20. 32 | Wild seris roots w/ pearl barley | draught | Benefit stomach |
| 0840 | Plin. 20. 32 | Seris | topical | Heart burn (applied above left breast) |
| 0841 | Plin. 20. 32 | Seris w/ vinegar | | Gout, spitting of blood, seminal flux |

| | | | | |
|---|---|---|---|---|
| 0842 | Plin. 20. 33 | Curly leaved cabbage (selinas) | | oral | Stomach and moderately laxative |
| 0843 | Plin. 20. 33 | Selinas | | oral | Headache |
| 0844 | Plin. 20. 33 | Selinas | | oral | Dimness of the eye |
| 0845 | Plin. 20. 33 | Selinas | | oral | Sparks in the eye |
| 0846 | Plin. 20. 33 | Selinas | | oral | Good for spleen |
| 0847 | Plin. 20. 33 | Selinas | | oral | Good for stomach |
| 0848 | Plin. 20. 33 | Selinas raw w/ oxymel, coriander, rue, mint and silphium root (2acetabula) (in morning) | | oral | Good for the hypochondria |
| 0849 | Plin. 20. 33 | Selinas w/ barley flour w/ dash or rue, coriander and salt | | liniment | Gout, rheumatic joints |
| 0850 | Plin. 20. 33 | Cabbage juice boiled down | | fomentation | Good for sinews and joints |
| 0851 | Plin. 20. 33 | Hot water | | fomentation | Wounds and cancerous sores |
| 0852 | Plin. 20. 33 | Pounded cabbage (twice daily) | | topical | Wounds and cancerous sores |
| 0853 | Plin. 20. 33 | 851 and 852 | | fomentation, topical | Fistulas and sprains |
| 0854 | Plin. 20. 33 | 851 and 852 | | fomentation, topical | Tumours |
| 0855 | Plin. 20. 33 | Boiled cabbage eaten fasting w/ oil and salt | | oral | Prevents dreams and sleeplessness |
| 0856 | Plin. 20. 33 | Cabbage boiled then boiled again w/ oil salt cumin and pearl barley | | oral | Gripings |
| 0857 | Plin. 20. 33 | Cabbage in dark wine | | drink | Clears bile |
| 0858 | Plin. 20. 33 | Warm urine of person on cabbage diet | | drink | Pains in the sinews |
| 0859 | Plin. 20. 33 | Warm urine of person on cabbage diet | | bath | Prevents children becoming weak |
| 0860 | Plin. 20. 33 | Cabbage juice w/ wine | | ear drops | Hardness of hearing and impetigo |
| 0861 | Plin. 20. 34 | Cabbage not overcooked | | oral | Bring away bile |
| 0862 | Plin. 20. 34 | Cabbage not overcooked | | oral | Loosens bowels |
| 0863 | Plin. 20. 34 | Cabbage boiled twice | | oral | Treats diarrhoea |
| 0864 | Plin. 20. 34 | Cabbage (food) | | oral | Prevents drunkenness |
| 0865 | Plin. 20. 34 | Cabbage (after drinking) | | oral | Dispels unpleasant effects of drinking |

| | | | | |
|---|---|---|---|---|
| 0866 | Plin. 20. 34 | Cabbage | oral | Brightens vision |
| 0867 | Plin. 20. 34 | Raw cabbage juice w/ attic honey | eye drops | Brightens vision touches the corner of eyes |
| 0868 | Plin. 20. 34 | Cabbage | oral | Clears the senses |
| 0869 | Plin. 20. 34 | Cabbage | oral | Good for stomach and sinews |
| 0870 | Plin. 20. 34 | Cabbage | oral | Paralysis, palsy and spitting blood |
| 0871 | Plin. 20. 34 | Cabbage boiled twice w/ salt | oral | Coeliac and dysentery |
| 0872 | Plin. 20. 34 | Cabbage boiled twice w/ salt | oral | Tenesmus and kidney troubles |
| 0873 | Plin. 20. 34 | Cabbage (food) | oral | Gave lactating women lots of milk |
| 0874 | Plin. 20. 34 | Cabbage (food) | oral | Aided woman's purgings |
| 0875 | Plin. 20. 34 | Cabbage stalk (raw) | oral | Brings out dead unborn baby |
| 0876 | Plin. 20. 34 | Cabbage seeds | oral | Antidote to poisonous fungi |
| 0877 | Plin. 20. 34 | Cabbage juice w/ wine | drunk | Antidote to poisonous fungi |
| 0878 | Plin. 20. 34 | Cabbage w/ goats milk, salt and honey | drink | Opisthonic tetanus |
| 0879 | Plin. 20. 34 | Cabbage (food) and cabbage water | oral | Gout |
| 0880 | Plin. 20. 34 | Cabbage water W/ salt | drink | Heartburn and epilepsy |
| 0881 | Plin. 20. 34 | Cabbage water w/ white wine (for forty days) | drink | Spleen ailments, jaundice and phrinitis |
| 0882 | Plin. 20. 34 | Juice of raw cabbage | gargle or drink | Hoarseness |
| 0883 | Plin. 20. 34 | Raw cabbage juice w/ vinegar, coriander, dill, honey and pepper | drink | Hiccoughs |
| 0884 | Plin. 20. 34 | Cabbage | | Flatulence of the stomach, snake bite, putrid sores (long term) |
| 0885 | Plin. 20. 34 | Cabbage water w/ barley meal | drink | Aching joints or gouty limbs |
| 0886 | Plin. 20. 34 | Cabbage juice w/ vinegar or fenugreek | drink | Aching joints or gouty limbs |
| 0887 | Plin. 20. 34 | 885, 886 | drink | Epinyctis and all other spreading eruptions |
| 0888 | Plin. 20. 34 | 885, 886 | drink | Sudden dimness of sight |
| 0889 | Plin. 20. 34 | Cabbage in vinegar | oral | Sudden dimness of sight |

| ID | Source | Preparation | Application | Use |
|---|---|---|---|---|
| 0890 | Plin. 20. 34 | Cabbage | topical | Bruises and livid marks |
| 0891 | Plin. 20. 34 | Cabbage in vinegar w/ a ball of alum | topical | Leprous sores and itch |
| 0892 | Plin. 20. 34 | Cabbage in vinegar w/ a ball of alum | topical | Prevents hair falling out |
| 0893 | Plin. 20. 34 | Cabbage | topical | Good for genitals and testis |
| 0894 | Plin. 20. 34 | Cabbage w/ beans | topical | Good for genitals and testis, and convulsions |
| 0895 | Plin. 20. 34 | Cabbage w/ rue | oral | High fever and stomach troubles |
| 0896 | Plin. 20. 34 | Cabbage w/ rue seed | oral | Bring away afterbirth |
| 0897 | Plin. 20. 34 | Cabbage w/ rue seed | oral | Antidote to shrew mouse bite |
| 0898 | Plin. 20. 34 | Dry cabbage leaves | oral | Purge by vomit or stool |
| 0899 | Plin. 20. 35 | Brussels sprouts | oral | Difficult to digest and bad for the kidneys |
| 0900 | Plin. 20. 35 | Ash from cabbage stalks w/ stale grease | | Sciatica |
| 0901 | Plin. 20. 35 | Ash from cabbage stalks w/ silphium and vinegar | depilatory | Prevents hair growth |
| 0902 | Plin. 20. 35 | Ash from cabbage lukewarm in oil | drink | Convulsions, internal ruptures and falls from a height |
| 0903 | Plin. 20. 35 | Ash from cabbage boiled in water | drink | Convulsions, internal ruptures and falls from a height |
| 0904 | Plin. 20. 35 | Cabbage | oral | Creates bad breath and harms the teeth and gums |
| 0905 | Plin. 20. 36 | Wild cabbage powder | snuff | Removes nose troubles and bad smells |
| 0906 | Plin. 20. 36 | Wild cabbage | oral | Flatulence, melancholy (illnesses of black bile) |
| 0907 | Plin. 20. 36 | Wild cabbage w/ honey (apply for 7 days) | topical | Fresh wounds |
| 0908 | Plin. 20. 36 | Wild cabbage in water | drink | Scrofula and fistula |
| 0909 | Plin. 20. 36 | Wild cabbage | oral | Running sores, removes excrescences and smooths scars |
| 0910 | Plin. 20. 36 | Wild cabbage | masticant | Sores in mouth and tonsils |
| 0911 | Plin. 20. 36 | Cabbage water w/ honey | gargle | Sores in mouth and tonsils |
| 0912 | Plin. 20. 36 | Three parts wild cabbage two parts alum in strong vinegar | liniment | Itch and chronic leprous sores |

| ID | Source | Preparation | Route | Use |
|---|---|---|---|---|
| 0913 | Plin. 20. 36 | Wild cabbage | topical | Mad dog bite |
| 0914 | Plin. 20. 36 | Wild cabbage w/ silphium juice and strong vinegar | topical | Mad dog bite |
| 0915 | Plin. 20. 36 | Wild cabbage seed roasted | oral | Helps against serpents fungi and bulls blood |
| 0916 | Plin. 20. 36 | Boiled wild cabbage leaves | oral | Diseases of the spleen and hardness of breasts |
| 0917 | Plin. 20. 36 | Raw wild cabbage leaves w/ sulphur and soda | oral | Diseases of the spleen and hardness of breasts |
| 0918 | Plin. 20. 36 | Ash of wild cabbage roots | topical | Swollen uvula, heals serpent bites |
| 0919 | Plin. 20. 36 | Ash of wild cabbage roots w/ honey | topical | Parotid swellings |
| 0920 | Plin. 20. 37 | Lapsana (a wild cabbage)(cooked) | oral | Loosens the bowels |
| 0921 | Plin. 20. 38 | Sea cabbage | oral | Strong purgative |
| 0922 | Plin. 20. 38 | Sea cabbage | oral | Bad for the stomach |
| 0923 | Plin. 20. 39 | Squill skinned and dried then plunged in vinegar for 48 days before solstice squills removed and vinegar stored | | |
| 0924 | Plin. 20. 39 | Squill vinegar | drink | Sharpens vision |
| 0925 | Plin. 20. 39 | Squill vinegar | drink | Beneficial for pains in stomach and sides if taken for 2 days |
| 0926 | Plin. 20. 39 | Too much squill vinegar | drink | Brings on the appearance of death |
| 0927 | Plin. 20. 39 | Squills alone | masticant | Good for the gums and teeth |
| 0928 | Plin. 20. 39 | Squills in vinegar and honey | oral | Tapeworm and other intestinal parasites |
| 0929 | Plin. 20. 39 | Fresh squills placed under the tongue | topical | Prevent dropsical patients suffering thirst |
| 0930 | Plin. 20. 39 | Dried raw squills boiled in vinegar | topical | Snake bites |
| 0931 | Plin. 20. 39 | Roast squills then clean then boil centres in water w/ honey and vinegar (3 oboli) | oral | Diuretic for dropsy, |
| 0932 | Plin. 20. 39 | Roast squills then clean then boil centres in water w/ honey and vinegar (3 oboli) | oral | Diseases of the spleen and stomach (w/ no ulceration) |
| 0933 | Plin. 20. 39 | Roast squills then clean then boil centres in water w/ honey and vinegar (3 oboli) | oral | Gripping pains, jaundice, chronic cough and asthma |
| 0934 | Plin. 20. 39 | Squill leaves (applied for 4 days) | topical | Scrofula |

| | | | | |
|---|---|---|---|---|
| 0935 | Plin. 20. 39 | Squills cooked in oil | topical | Dandruff and running sores |
| 0936 | Plin. 20. 39 | Squills cooked in honey | oral | Digestion |
| 0937 | Plin. 20. 39 | Squills cooked in honey | oral | Purge the bowels |
| 0938 | Plin. 20. 39 | Squills cooked in oil and mixed w/ resin | topical | Cracks in the feet |
| 0939 | Plin. 20. 39 | Squill seed w/ honey | topical | Lumbago |
| 0940 | Plin. 20. 39 | Squills hung in doorway | folk | Keep off evil enchantments |
| 0941 | Plin. 20. 40 | Bulbs w/ vinegar and sulphur | topical | Cuts on the face |
| 0942 | Plin. 20. 40 | Bulbs pounded | topical | Contraction of the sinews |
| 0943 | Plin. 20. 40 | Bulbs pounded w/ wine | | Dandruff |
| 0944 | Plin. 20. 40 | Bulbs pounded w/ honey or pitch | topical | The bites of dogs |
| 0945 | Plin. 20. 40 | Bulbs w/ honey | topical | Stop bleeding |
| 0946 | Plin. 20. 40 | Bulbs w/ coriander and flour | topical | Nosebleed |
| 0947 | Plin. 20. 40 | Bulbs in vinegar | drink | Lichen |
| 0948 | Plin. 20. 40 | Bulbs in vinegar w/ dry wine or egg | drink | Eruptions on the head |
| 0949 | Plin. 20. 40 | Bulbs | topical | Eye fluxes |
| 0950 | Plin. 20. 40 | Bulb centres | topical | Dry ophthalmia |
| 0951 | Plin. 20. 40 | Red bulbs w/honey and soda (in the sun) | topical | Remove spots on the face |
| 0952 | Plin. 20. 40 | Red bulbs w/wine or vinegar (in the sun) | topical | Removes freckles |
| 0953 | Plin. 20. 40 | Bulbs | topical | Wounds |
| 0954 | Plin. 20. 40 | Bulbs w/ honey wine (applied for a minimum of 4 days) | topical | Wounds |
| 0955 | Plin. 20. 40 | Bulbs w/ honey wine (applied for a minimum of 4 days) | topical | Broken ear-laps and hydrocele |
| 0956 | Plin. 20. 40 | Bulbs w/ honey wine and flour (applied for a minimum of 4 days) | topical | Joint pains |
| 0957 | Plin. 20. 40 | Bulbs boiled applied to belly | topical | Soften hard abdomen |
| 0958 | Plin. 20. 40 | Bulbs w/ wine and diluted rain water | drink | Dysentery |
| 0959 | Plin. 20. 40 | Bulbs w/ silphium (pills the size of a bean) | pill | Internal spasms |
| 0960 | Plin. 20. 40 | Bulbs bruised | topical | Sweating |

| | | | | |
|---|---|---|---|---|
| 0961 | Plin. 20. 40 | Bulbs | oral | Good for sinews, paralytics |
| 0962 | Plin. 20. 40 | Red bulbs w/ honey and salt | | Heal sprains of the foot quickly |
| 0963 | Plin. 20. 40 | Megarian bulbs | oral | Strong aphrodisiac |
| 0964 | Plin. 20. 40 | Garden bulbs w/ concentrated must or raisin wine | oral | Aid delivery |
| 0965 | Plin. 20. 40 | Wiled bulbs w/ silphium | pill | Intestinal worms or afflictions |
| 0966 | Plin. 20. 40 | Wild bulb seed w/ wine | drink | Venomous spiders |
| 0967 | Plin. 20. 40 | Bulbs in vinegar | topical | Snake bites |
| 0968 | Plin. 20. 40 | Bulb seed (to drink) | drink | Raving mad |
| 0969 | Plin. 20. 40 | Bulb flowers pounded | topical | Spots on the leg and patches created by fire |
| 0970 | Plin. 20. 40 | Bulbs | oral | Weakens eye |
| 0971 | Plin. 20. 40 | Bulbs | oral | Difficult to digest |
| 0972 | Plin. 20. 41 | Bulbine | topical | Recent wounds |
| 0973 | Plin. 20. 41 | Emetic' bulb | oral | Emetic |
| 0974 | Plin. 20. 42 | Asparagus | oral | Good for stomach |
| 0975 | Plin. 20. 42 | Asparagus w/ cumin | oral | Flatulence of the stomach and colon |
| 0976 | Plin. 20. 42 | Asparagus w/ cumin cooked in wine | oral | Improves vision moves the bowels gently, benefits pains in the chest and spine and intestinal trouble |
| 0977 | Plin. 20. 42 | Asparagus seed (3 oboli) w/ equal cumin in drink | drink | Pains in loins and kidneys |
| 0978 | Plin. 20. 42 | Asparagus | oral | Aphrodisiac |
| 0979 | Plin. 20. 42 | Asparagus | oral | Diuretic (except when bladder is ulcerated) |
| 0980 | Plin. 20. 42 | Asparagus roots pounded w/ white wine | drink | Disperses stone and pain in loins and kidneys |
| 0981 | Plin. 20. 42 | Asparagus root in sweet wine | drink | Pain in the womb |
| 0982 | Plin. 20. 42 | Root boiled in vinegar | oral | Elephantiasis |
| 0983 | Plin. 20. 42 | Pounded asparagus and oil | bath | Never stung by bees |
| 0984 | Plin. 20. 43 | Wild asparagus | oral | Relieve jaundice |

| | | | | |
|---|---|---|---|---|
| 0985 | Plin. 20. 43 | Wild asparagus water decoction (up to a hemina) | drink | Aphrodisiac |
| 0986 | Plin. 20. 43 | Wild asparagus seed w/ dill (3 oboli) | oral | Aphrodisiac |
| 0987 | Plin. 20. 43 | Decoction of wild asparagus juice | drink | Snake bites |
| 0988 | Plin. 20. 43 | Wild asparagus root w/ fennel root | | Not listed |
| 0989 | Plin. 20. 43 | Asparagus, parsley and cumin seed (3oboli) in wine (2 cyathi) | oral | Haematuria |
| 0990 | Plin. 20. 43 | Asparagus, parsley and cumin seed (3oboli) in wine (2 cyathi) | oral | Diuretic |
| 0991 | Plin. 20. 43 | Asparagus, parsley and cumin seed (3oboli) in wine (2 cyathi) | oral | Bad for dropsy and venery and the bladder (unless boiled) |
| 0992 | Plin. 20. 43 | Asparagus root juice boiled in wine (held in mouth) | gargle | Toothache |
| 0993 | Plin. 20. 44 | Parsley w/ honey | eye drops | Eye fluxes |
| 0994 | Plin. 20. 44 | Parsley decoction | fomentation | Flux of the limbs |
| 0995 | Plin. 20. 44 | Parsley pounded or w/ bread or pearl barley | poultice | Flux of the limbs |
| 0996 | Plin. 20. 44 | Parsley | oral | Bad for eyesight |
| 0997 | Plin. 20. 44 | If female parsley is eaten | oral | Makes eater (of either sex) barren |
| 0998 | Plin. 20. 44 | If nurse eats female parsley | oral | Babies become epileptic |
| 0999 | Plin. 20. 44 | Application of (m) parsley leaves | topical | Softens hardness of the breasts |
| 1000 | Plin. 20. 44 | Juice of parsley roots w/ wine | drink | Lumbago |
| 1001 | Plin. 20. 44 | Juice of parsley roots w/ wine | ear drops | Hardness of hearing |
| 1002 | Plin. 20. 44 | Parsley seed | oral | Diuretic |
| 1003 | Plin. 20. 44 | Parsley seed | oral | Aids the menses and the afterbirth |
| 1004 | Plin. 20. 44 | Parsley seed decoction | fomentation | Restores bruises to their natural colour |
| 1005 | Plin. 20. 44 | Parsley w/ egg white | drink | Kidney troubles |
| 1006 | Plin. 20. 44 | Parsley boiled | drink | Kidney troubles |
| 1007 | Plin. 20. 44 | Parsley pounded in cold water | drink | Mouth ulcers |
| 1008 | Plin. 20. 44 | Parsley seed in wine | drink | Bladder stones |
| 1009 | Plin. 20. 44 | Parsley root w/ old wine | drink | Bladder stones |

| | | | | |
|---|---|---|---|---|
| 1010 | Plin. 20. 44 | Parsley seed w/ white wine | drink | Jaundice |
| 1011 | Plin. 20. 46 | Alexanders seed in drink | drink | Colic and intestinal worms |
| 1012 | Plin. 20. 46 | Seed boiled w/ honey wine | drink | Dysuria |
| 1013 | Plin. 20. 46 | Alexander rood boiled in wine | drink | Stones, lumbago and pains in the side |
| 1014 | Plin. 20. 46 | Alexander taken in drink and as a liniment | drink and liniment | Bite of a mad dog |
| 1015 | Plin. 20. 46 | Alexander juice | drink | Warms those who have been chilled |
| 1016 | Plin. 20. 46 | Mountain parsley | oral | Aids urination and menses |
| 1017 | Plin. 20. 46 | Wild celery | | Spider bites |
| 1018 | Plin. 20. 46 | Wild celery and mountain parsley w/ wine | drink | Promotes menses |
| 1019 | Plin. 20. 47 | Rock parsley juice (2 spoonful's) w/ juice of horehound (1 cyath) and warm water (3 cyaths) | drink | Abscesses |
| 1020 | Plin. 20. 47 | Cow parsley in drink or topical | drink, topical | Antidote to snake bites |
| 1021 | Plin. 20. 48 | Ocimum (basil) | oral | Bad for stomach urine and eyesight |
| 1022 | Plin. 20. 48 | Ocimum (basil) | | Causes madness lethargies and liver troubles |
| 1023 | Plin. 20. 48 | Ocimum (basil) | | Breeds pestilent animals |
| 1024 | Plin. 20. 48 | Ocimum (basil) | | Amplifies scorpion venom |
| 1025 | Plin. 20. 48 | Ocimum (basil) w/ wine and a little vinegar | drink | Cures scorpion stings |
| 1026 | Plin. 20. 48 | Ocimum (basil) smelt in vinegar | smell | Good for fainting, lethargies and cooling inflammations |
| 1027 | Plin. 20. 48 | Ocimum (basil) w/ rose or myrtle oil or vinegar | liniment | Headache |
| 1028 | Plin. 20. 48 | Ocimum (basil) w/ wine | eye drops | Eye fluxes |
| 1029 | Plin. 20. 48 | Ocimum (basil) w/ vinegar | oral | Good for stomach, dispels belching |
| 1030 | Plin. 20. 48 | Ocimum (basil) | topical | Dispels looseness of bowels |
| 1031 | Plin. 20. 48 | Ocimum (basil) | oral | Diuretic, jaundice and dropsy |
| 1032 | Plin. 20. 48 | Ocimum (basil) | oral | Diarrhoea of cholera |
| 1033 | Plin. 20. 48 | Ocimum (basil) | oral | Coeliac complaints |

| | | | | |
|---|---|---|---|---|
| 1034 | Plin. 20. 48 | Ocimum (basil) boiled | oral | Dysentery |
| 1035 | Plin. 20. 48 | Ocimum (basil) w/ wine | drink | Tenesmus, spitting blood and hardness of the hypochondria |
| 1036 | Plin. 20. 48 | Ocimum (basil) on breast | topical | Stops lactation |
| 1037 | Plin. 20. 48 | Ocimum (basil) w/ goose grease | ear drops | The ears of babies |
| 1038 | Plin. 20. 48 | Ocimum (basil) seed pounded in nostril | snuff | Promotes sneezing |
| 1039 | Plin. 20. 48 | Ocimum (basil) | liniment | Promotes mucus from the head |
| 1040 | Plin. 20. 48 | Ocimum (basil) w/ vinegar | oral | Purges womb |
| 1041 | Plin. 20. 48 | Ocimum (basil) w/ cobblers blacking | topical | Removes warts |
| 1042 | Plin. 20. 48 | Ocimum (basil) | | Veterinary uses |
| 1043 | Plin. 20. 48 | Wild basil root | | Bites of wild beasts |
| 1044 | Plin. 20. 49 | Rocket seed | oral | Poison of scorpions and shrew mouse |
| 1045 | Plin. 20. 49 | Rocket | bath | Keeps of bodily parasites |
| 1046 | Plin. 20. 49 | Rocket w/ honey | topical | Removes spots of the face |
| 1047 | Plin. 20. 49 | Rocket w/ vinegar | topical | Removes freckles |
| 1048 | Plin. 20. 49 | Rocket w/ ox gall | topical | Reduces livid scares to whiteness |
| 1049 | Plin. 20. 49 | Rocket w/ wine | drink | Harden (body) |
| 1050 | Plin. 20. 49 | Rocket slightly pounded | fomentation | Clears vision |
| 1051 | Plin. 20. 49 | Rocket (*lacuna) | | Coughing of babies |
| 1052 | Plin. 20. 49 | Rocket decoction | | Extracts broken bones |
| 1053 | Plin. 20. 49 | Rocket (3 leaves) (plucked with the left hand)pounded w/ hydromel | drink | Aphrodisiac |
| 1054 | Plin. 20. 50 | Cress | oral | Counter aphrodisiac |
| 1055 | Plin. 20. 50 | White cress (1 denarius) w/ water (7 denarius) | drink | Purge, removes bile |
| 1056 | Plin. 20. 50 | White cress w/ bean meal and covered in cabbage leaf | oral | Scrofula |
| 1057 | Plin. 20. 50 | Dark cress | oral | Purges humours of the head; clears the vision |
| 1058 | Plin. 20. 50 | Dark cress w/ vinegar | oral | Calms troubled minds |

| | | | | |
|---|---|---|---|---|
| 1059 | Plin. 20. 50 | Dark cress w/ wine or a fig | oral | Benefits the spleen |
| 1060 | Plin. 20. 50 | Dark cress w/ honey (daily on empty stomach) | oral | Cough |
| 1061 | Plin. 20. 50 | Cress seed | oral | Intestinal parasites |
| 1062 | Plin. 20. 50 | Cress seed w/ wild mint | oral | Intestinal parasites |
| 1063 | Plin. 20. 50 | Cress w/ wild marjoram and sweet wine | drink | Asthma and cough |
| 1064 | Plin. 20. 50 | Cress decoction in goats milk | drink | Relieves chest pains |
| 1065 | Plin. 20. 50 | Cress w/ pitch | plaster | Superficial abscesses |
| 1066 | Plin. 20. 50 | Cress w/ vinegar | topical | Extracts thorns and removes spots |
| 1067 | Plin. 20. 50 | Cress w/ egg white | | Carcinoma |
| 1068 | Plin. 20. 50 | Cress w/ vinegar (on spleen) | topical | Spleen |
| 1069 | Plin. 20. 50 | Cress w/ vinegar in honey (for babies) (on spleen) | topical | Spleen |
| 1070 | Plin. 20. 50 | Burnt cress | topical | Deters serpents and neutralises scorpion stings |
| 1071 | Plin. 20. 50 | Pounded cress | | Headache |
| 1072 | Plin. 20. 50 | Pounded cress w/ mustard | | Mange |
| 1073 | Plin. 20. 50 | Cress pounded w/ fig | topical | Hardness of hearing |
| 1074 | Plin. 20. 50 | Cress juice (poured in ears) | ear drops | Toothache |
| 1075 | Plin. 20. 50 | Cress juice w/ goose grease | topical | Dandruff and sores of the head |
| 1076 | Plin. 20. 50 | Cress w/ leaven | topical | Brings boils to a head |
| 1077 | Plin. 20. 50 | Cress | topical | Makes carbuncles suppurate and break |
| 1078 | Plin. 20. 50 | Cress w/ honey | topical | Cleanses phagedaenic ulcers |
| 1079 | Plin. 20. 50 | Cress w/ pearl barley and vinegar | topical | Sciatica and lumbago |
| 1080 | Plin. 20. 50 | Cress w/ pearl barley and vinegar | topical | Lichen and rough nails |
| 1081 | Plin. 20. 51 | Rue juice extracted by pounding with a little water and store in a copper box | drink | Overdose is poisonous |
| 1082 | Plin. 20. 51 | Hemlock juice | drink | Antidote to rue juice |
| 1083 | Plin. 20. 51 | | topical | Good for the hands and face of rue gatherers |

| | | | | |
|---|---|---|---|---|
| 1084 | Plin. 20. 51 | Pounded rue leaves w/ wine | drink | Antidote aconite and mistletoe |
| 1085 | Plin. 20. 51 | Rue | oral | Poisonous fungi |
| 1086 | Plin. 20. 51 | Rue | oral | Protects against snake bites |
| 1087 | Plin. 20. 51 | Rue | topical | Scorpion, spiders, bees, hornets and wasps stings |
| 1088 | Plin. 20. 51 | Rue | topical | Cantharides and salamander injuries and bites of mad dog |
| 1089 | Plin. 20. 51 | Rue juice /w wine (1 acetabulum) w/ rue leaves pounded or chewed w/ honey or salt | oral | |
| 1090 | Plin. 20. 51 | Rue leaves boiled w/ vinegar and pitch | oral | Never stung by poisonous creatures |
| 1091 | Plin. 20. 51 | Smeared w/ rue juice or having it on their person | bath | Snakes avoid smell |
| 1092 | Plin. 20. 51 | Burning rue | fumigation | |
| 1093 | Plin. 20. 51 | Wild rue root w/ wine | drink | Most powerful form |
| 1094 | Plin. 20. 51 | Draught more effective if taken outside | | |
| 1095 | Plin. 20. 51 | Rue | oral | Good for the eyes |
| 1096 | Plin. 20. 51 | Rue juice w/ attic honey or milk of women who has born a male or straight | eye drops | Dim vision |
| 1097 | Plin. 20. 51 | Rue w/ pearl barley | eye drops | Eye fluxes |
| 1098 | Plin. 20. 51 | Rue w/ wine or vinegar and rose oil | drink | Headache |
| 1099 | Plin. 20. 51 | Rue w/ wine or vinegar and rose oil w/ barley flour and vinegar | drink | Headache (chronic) |
| 1100 | Plin. 20. 51 | Rue | oral | Indigestion, flatulence, chronic pains of the stomach |
| 1101 | Plin. 20. 51 | Rue w/ honey (on abdomen and chest) | oral | Opens the womb and corrects displacement of it |
| 1102 | Plin. 20. 51 | Rue w/ figs boiled down to a half w/ wine | drink | Dropsy |
| 1103 | Plin. 20. 51 | Rue w/ figs boiled down to a half w/ wine | drink | Pains in chest, side and loin; coughs asthma |
| 1104 | Plin. 20. 51 | Rue w/ figs boiled down to a half w/ wine | drink | Complaints of lung liver and kidneys and cold shivers |
| 1105 | Plin. 20. 51 | Rue leaf decoction | drink | Prevents hangover |
| 1106 | Plin. 20. 51 | Rue (food) boiled in hyssop w/ wine | oral | Colic |

| | | | | |
|---|---|---|---|---|
| 1107 | Plin. 20. 51 | Rue (food) boiled in hyssop w/ wine | oral | Stops internal haemorrhage |
| 1108 | Plin. 20. 51 | Rue boiled in hyssop w/ wine | injection | Stops nosebleed |
| 1109 | Plin. 20. 51 | Rue boiled in hyssop w/ wine | gargle | Rinsing teeth |
| 1110 | Plin. 20. 51 | Rue juice | ear drops | Ear ache |
| 1111 | Plin. 20. 51 | Rue juice w/ rose oil or baby oil or wine and honey | ear drops | Hardness of hearing or ringing in ears |
| 1112 | Plin. 20. 51 | Rue juice w/ vinegar (poured over cranium and temples) | topical | Phrenitis |
| 1113 | Plin. 20. 51 | Rue juice w/ vinegar wild thyme and bay (poured over cranium and temples) | topical | Phrenitis |
| 1114 | Plin. 20. 51 | Rue w/ vinegar | smell | Lethargies |
| 1115 | Plin. 20. 51 | Rue juice (4 cyaths) | drink | Epilepsy |
| 1116 | Plin. 20. 51 | Rue | oral | Fever |
| 1117 | Plin. 20. 51 | Rue raw | oral | Shivering fits |
| 1118 | Plin. 20. 51 | Rue | oral | Diuretic |
| 1119 | Plin. 20. 51 | Rue w/ sweet dark wine (drink or topical) | drink or topical | Promotes menstruation, brings away placenta and dead foetus |
| 1120 | Plin. 20. 51 | Rue | fumigation | Stimulate the womb |
| 1121 | Plin. 20. 51 | Rue w/ vinegar, barley and honey | oral | Heart burn |
| 1122 | Plin. 20. 51 | Rue w/ vinegar honey and barley boiled in oil and spread over fleece | oral | Sever colic |
| 1123 | Plin. 20. 51 | Dried rue (2 drachma) sulphur (1 1/2 drachma) | oral | Purulent spittings |
| 1124 | Plin. 20. 51 | 3 sprays boiled in wine | oral | Spitting blood |
| 1125 | Plin. 20. 51 | Rue pounded w/ wine and cheese | oral | Dysentery |
| 1126 | Plin. 20. 51 | Crumbled in draught w/ bitumen | oral | Shortness of breath |
| 1127 | Plin. 20. 51 | Rue seed (3 oz.) Oil (1 pound) wine (1 sextrarus) | drink | Heavy falls |
| 1128 | Plin. 20. 51 | Rue leaves boiled in oil | topical | Frostbite |
| 1129 | Plin. 20. 51 | Rue | oral | Urinal incontinence |
| 1130 | Plin. 20. 51 | Rue w/ honey and alum | oral | Itch and leprous sores |

| | | | | |
|---|---|---|---|---|
| 1131 | Plin. 20. 51 | Rue w/ nightshade lard and beef suet | oral | Vitiligo, warts, and scrofula |
| 1132 | Plin. 20. 51 | Rue w/ vinegar, oil or white lead | | Erysipelas |
| 1133 | Plin. 20. 51 | Rue w/ vinegar | | Carbuncles |
| 1134 | Plin. 20. 51 | Rue w/ vinegar and silphium | topical | Night pustules |
| 1135 | Plin. 20. 51 | Rue decoction | topical | Swollen breasts |
| 1136 | Plin. 20. 51 | Rue decoction w/ wax | | Phlegm outbursts |
| 1137 | Plin. 20. 51 | Rue w/ tender sprigs of laurel | topical | Testicular flux |
| 1138 | Plin. 20. 51 | Wild rue w/ old axle grease | topical | Hernia |
| 1139 | Plin. 20. 51 | Rue seed w/ wax | topical | Broken limbs |
| 1140 | Plin. 20. 51 | Rue root | topical | Blood shot eyes, scars and spots |
| 1141 | Plin. 20. 51 | Rue boiled in rose oil w/ (1 oz.) Aloe | bath | Antiperspirant |
| 1142 | Plin. 20. 51 | Rue | oral | Spermatorrhoea and amorous dreams |
| 1143 | Plin. 20. 51 | Rue | oral | Kills foetus |
| 1144 | Plin. 20. 51 | Rue | | Veterinary uses |
| 1145 | Plin. 20. 51 | Nasal injection w/ wine or vinegar | injection | Quadruped has swallowed a bloodsucker |
| 1146 | Plin. 20. 52 | Wild mint leaves | masticant, topical | Elephantiasis |
| 1147 | Plin. 20. 52 | Wild mint leaves (2 drachmi) in wine (2 cyaths) | drink or topical | Snake bites |
| 1148 | Plin. 20. 52 | Wild mint leaves (2 drachmi) in wine (2 cyaths) w/ salt, oil and vinegar | drink or topical | Scorpion stings |
| 1149 | Plin. 20. 52 | Wild mint juice | decoction | Scopendra |
| 1150 | Plin. 20. 52 | Wild mint leaves dried and powdered | oral | Antidote to poisons |
| 1151 | Plin. 20. 52 | Wild mint in drink brings about menstruation | drink | Brings on menstruation and kills the foetus |
| 1152 | Plin. 20. 52 | Wild mint | oral | Ruptures spasms orthopnoea colic and cholera |
| 1153 | Plin. 20. 52 | Wild mint | topical | Lumbago and gout |
| 1154 | Plin. 20. 52 | Wild mint juice | ear injection | Ear parasites |

| | | | | | |
|---|---|---|---|---|---|
| 1155 | Plin. 20. 52 | Wild mint in drink | | drink | Jaundice |
| 1156 | Plin. 20. 52 | Wild mint | | ointment | Scrofula |
| 1157 | Plin. 20. 52 | Wild mint | | oral | Prevents amorous dreams |
| 1158 | Plin. 20. 52 | Wild mint w/ vinegar | | drink | Expels worms |
| 1159 | Plin. 20. 52 | Wild mint w/ vinegar poured over the head in the sun | | topical | Dandruff |
| 1160 | Plin. 20. 53 | Mint w/ water or honey wine | | drink | People chocked by curdled draught |
| 1161 | Plin. 20. 53 | Mint | | oral | Stops bleeding in both genders including menstrual flux |
| 1162 | Plin. 20. 53 | Mint w/ water and starch | | drink | Stops violent disturbance of the bowels |
| 1163 | Plin. 20. 53 | Mint | | topical | Ulceration and abscesses of the womb |
| 1164 | Plin. 20. 53 | Mint (3 oboli) w/ honey wine | | oral | Liver complaints, spitting blood |
| 1165 | Plin. 20. 53 | Mint | | topical | Sores on children's head |
| 1166 | Plin. 20. 53 | Mint | | oral | Dries a wet and braces a dry trachea |
| 1167 | Plin. 20. 53 | Mint w/ honey wine and water | | drink | Clears purulent phlegm |
| 1168 | Plin. 20. 53 | Mint juice | | drink | Benefits the voice before strain |
| 1169 | Plin. 20. 53 | Mint juice w/ coriander rue and milk | | gargle | Swollen uvula |
| 1170 | Plin. 20. 53 | Mint w/ alum | | oral | Tonsils |
| 1171 | Plin. 20. 53 | Mint w/ honey | | oral | A rough tongue |
| 1172 | Plin. 20. 53 | Mint | | oral | Internal spasms and lung complaints |
| 1173 | Plin. 20. 53 | Mint w/ pomegranate juice | | drink | Hiccoughs and vomiting |
| 1174 | Plin. 20. 53 | Mint juice | | fumigation | Infections of the nostrils |
| 1175 | Plin. 20. 53 | Mint pounded | | topical | Cholera |
| 1176 | Plin. 20. 53 | Mint w/ vinegar | | drink | Internal bleeding |
| 1177 | Plin. 20. 53 | Mint w/ pearl barley | | plaster | Iliac troubles and tensions of the breasts |
| 1178 | Plin. 20. 53 | Mint on temples | | topical | Headache |
| 1179 | Plin. 20. 53 | Mint | | topical | Scolopendra, sea scorpion and serpent |

| | | | | |
|---|---|---|---|---|
| 1180 | Plin. 20. 53 | Mint | topical | Eye fluxes, head eruptions, rectal troubles |
| 1181 | Plin. 20. 53 | Mint (when held in the hand) | topical | Chafing |
| 1182 | Plin. 20. 53 | Mint w/ honey wine | ear drops | |
| 1183 | Plin. 20. 53 | Eaten from garden without picking (for 9 days) | oral | Spleen problems |
| 1184 | Plin. 20. 53 | Mint powder (three fingered pinch) w/ water | drink | Stomach ache |
| 1185 | Plin. 20. 53 | Mint powder (3 fingered pinch) w/ drink | drink | Expels worms |
| 1186 | Plin. 20. 54 | Mint and pennyroyal w/ vinegar | smell | Reviving the fainted |
| 1187 | Plin. 20. 54 | Pennyroyal | topical | Headache |
| 1188 | Plin. 20. 54 | Pennyroyal | smell | Prevents headache thirst, susceptibility to heat or cold |
| 1189 | Plin. 20. 54 | Pennyroyal w/ pearl barley and vinegar | topical | Pains |
| 1190 | Plin. 20. 54 | Pennyroyal w/ cold water, salt and pearl barley | drink | Checks nausea |
| 1191 | Plin. 20. 54 | Pennyroyal w/ cold water, salt and pearl barley | drink | Pains in the chest |
| 1192 | Plin. 20. 54 | Pennyroyal w/ cold water | drink | Stomach pains |
| 1193 | Plin. 20. 54 | Pennyroyal in vinegar and pearl barley | oral | Gnawing and vomiting |
| 1194 | Plin. 20. 54 | Pennyroyal in salt, vinegar and pearl barley | oral | Loosens the bowels |
| 1195 | Plin. 20. 54 | Pennyroyal boiled w/ honey and soda | oral | Complaints of the intestines |
| 1196 | Plin. 20. 54 | Pennyroyal w/ wine | drink | Diuretic |
| 1197 | Plin. 20. 54 | Pennyroyal w/ Armenian wine | drink | Disperses stone and all internal pain |
| 1198 | Plin. 20. 54 | Pennyroyal w/ honey and vinegar | oral | Relives menstruation and afterbirth |
| 1199 | Plin. 20. 54 | Pennyroyal w/ honey and vinegar | oral | Hysteria |
| 1200 | Plin. 20. 54 | Pennyroyal w/ honey and vinegar | oral | Expels dead foetus |
| 1201 | Plin. 20. 54 | Pennyroyal seed | smell | Aphasia |
| 1202 | Plin. 20. 54 | Pennyroyal seed w/ vinegar (1 cyahtus) | drink | Epilepsy |
| 1203 | Plin. 20. 54 | Pennyroyal w/ unwholesome water | drink | Water purification |
| 1204 | Plin. 20. 54 | Pennyroyal w /wine | drink | Relieves tiredness |

| # | Ref | Substance | Application | Use |
|---|---|---|---|---|
| 1205 | Plin. 20. 54 | Pennyroyal w/ salt and vinegar (rubbed on sinews) | bath | Sinews when cramped |
| 1206 | Plin. 20. 54 | Pennyroyal w/ honey | | Opisthotonic tetanus |
| 1207 | Plin. 20. 54 | Pennyroyal decoction | drink | Serpent bites |
| 1208 | Plin. 20. 54 | Pennyroyal w/ wine (especially if grown in dry soil) | drink | Stings of scorpions |
| 1209 | Plin. 20. 54 | Pennyroyal | oral | Ulceration of the mouth and cough |
| 1210 | Plin. 20. 54 | Pennyroyal flower (burnt) | fumigation | Kills fleas |
| 1211 | Plin. 20. 54 | Pennyroyal in wool | smell | Tertian ague (before fever) |
| 1212 | Plin. 20. 54 | Pennyroyal (placed under bed clothes | smell | Tertian ague (before fever) |
| 1213 | Plin. 20. 55 | Wild pennyroyal (dittany) rubbed | bath | Patients w/ chill rubbed before a bath |
| 1214 | Plin. 20. 55 | Wild pennyroyal (dittany) rubbed | bath | Ague (before shivering fits) |
| 1215 | Plin. 20. 55 | Wild pennyroyal | oral | Convulsions gripping of bowels and gout |
| 1216 | Plin. 20. 55 | Wild pennyroyal w/ honey and salt | drink | Cramps |
| 1217 | Plin. 20. 55 | Wild pennyroyal | oral | Makes expectoration easier w/ lung troubles |
| 1218 | Plin. 20. 55 | Wild pennyroyal w/ salt | oral | Spleen troubles, bladder asthma and flatulence |
| 1219 | Plin. 20. 55 | Wild pennyroyal decoction or juice | drink | Hysteria heals scolipendra wound, scorpion and Man bite |
| 1220 | Plin. 20. 55 | Wild pennyroyal root fresh | topical | Spreading ulcers |
| 1221 | Plin. 20. 55 | Wild pennyroyal root dry | topical | Restores the colour of scars |
| 1222 | Plin. 20. 56 | Pennyroyal and catmint (boiled to 1/3) | drink | Disperse chills, help menstruation and allay the heats of summer |
| 1223 | Plin. 20. 56 | Catmint | oral | Antidote to snake bites |
| 1224 | Plin. 20. 56 | Catmint burning | fumigation | Deters snakes |
| 1225 | Plin. 20. 56 | Catmint under bedclothes | small | Deters snakes |
| 1226 | Plin. 20. 56 | Catmint | topical | Lachrymal fistula |
| 1227 | Plin. 20. 56 | Fresh catmint w/ 1/3 part bread in vinegar | liniment | Headache |
| 1228 | Plin. 20. 56 | Catmint juice | nose drops | Nosebleed |

| | | | | |
|---|---|---|---|---|
| 1229 | Plin. 20. 56 | Catmint root w/ myrtle seeds and warm raisin wine | gargle | Quinsy |
| 1230 | Plin. 20. 57 | Wild cumin | oral | Stomach trouble |
| 1231 | Plin. 20. 57 | Wild cumin pounded w/ bread | oral | Dispels phlegm or flatulence |
| 1232 | Plin. 20. 57 | Wild cumin w/ water or wine | drink | Dispels phlegm or flatulence |
| 1233 | Plin. 20. 57 | 1231 and 1232 | | Gripping and pains in the bowels |
| 1234 | Plin. 20. 57 | Cumin | | Produces paleness |
| 1235 | Plin. 20. 57 | Wild cumin lozenges or fresh in vinegar | topical | Nosebleed |
| 1236 | Plin. 20. 57 | Wild cumin | topical | Fluxes of the eyes |
| 1237 | Plin. 20. 57 | Wild cumin w/ honey | topical | Swollen eyes |
| 1238 | Plin. 20. 57 | Wild cumin w/ honey (on abdomen for babies) | topical | Swollen eyes |
| 1239 | Plin. 20. 57 | Wild cumin w/ white wine (after bathing) | drink | Jaundice |
| 1240 | Plin. 20. 57 | Ethiopian cumin w/ vinegar and water | drink | Incontinence of urine |
| 1241 | Plin. 20. 57 | Ethiopian cumin w/ honey | electuary | Incontinence of urine |
| 1242 | Plin. 20. 57 | Cumin (parched) and beaten w/ vinegar | drink | Liver troubles and vertigo |
| 1243 | Plin. 20. 57 | Cumin crushed w/ sweet wine | drink | Over acrid urine |
| 1244 | Plin. 20. 57 | Cumin in wine | drink | Uterine disorders |
| 1245 | Plin. 20. 57 | Cumin leaves in wool | topical | Uterine disorders |
| 1246 | Plin. 20. 57 | Cumin dried (crushed) w/ honey, rose oil or wax | topical | Swollen testis |
| 1247 | Plin. 20. 57 | Wild cumin w/ oil | topical | Bites of serpents, scorpions or scolopendras |
| 1248 | Plin. 20. 57 | Cumin (3 finger pinch) w/ wine | drink | Vomiting and nausea |
| 1249 | Plin. 20. 57 | Cumin (3 finger pinch) w/ wine | drink | Colic |
| 1250 | Plin. 20. 57 | Cumin (hot) in lint held in place w/ bandages | topical | Colic |
| 1251 | Plin. 20. 57 | Cumin (3 drachmae) w/ wine (3 cyaths) | drink | Opens up suffocation of the womb |
| 1252 | Plin. 20. 57 | Cumin w/ veal suet or honey | ear drops | Ringing or noises in ear |
| 1253 | Plin. 20. 57 | Cumin w/ honey raisins and vinegar | topical | Bruises |
| 1254 | Plin. 20. 57 | Cumin w/ vinegar | topical | Black freckles |

| # | Ref | Substance | Method | Use |
|---|---|---|---|---|
| 1255 | Plin. 20. 58 | Ami (like cumin) | | Dispels flatulence and gripping |
| 1256 | Plin. 20. 58 | Ami (like cumin) | | Promotes urine and menstruation |
| 1257 | Plin. 20. 58 | Ami (like cumin) | | Relieves bruises and fluxes of the eye |
| 1258 | Plin. 20. 58 | Ami (like cumin) w/ linseed and wine (2 drachmi) | drink | Scorpion wounds |
| 1259 | Plin. 20. 58 | Ami (like cumin) w/ linseed and wine and myrrh (equal) (2 drachmi) | drink | Cerastes bite |
| 1260 | Plin. 20. 58 | Ami (like cumin) | | Makes users pale |
| 1261 | Plin. 20. 58 | Ami (like cumin) w/ raisons or resin | fumigation | Purge of womb |
| 1262 | Plin. 20. 58 | Ami (like cumin) (smelt during intercourse) | smell | More easily conceive |
| 1263 | Plin. 20. 59 | Capers (daily) | oral | Prevents paralysis and pains of the spleen |
| 1264 | Plin. 20. 59 | Caper root crushed and rubbed on skin in sun | bath | Removes white eruptions |
| 1265 | Plin. 20. 59 | Skin of the caper root (2 drachma) w/ wine (not permitted to bathe) | drink | Spleen troubles |
| 1266 | Plin. 20. 59 | Capper in drink | drink | Lumbago and paralysis |
| 1267 | Plin. 20. 59 | Caper seed pounded in vinegar | drink | Toothache |
| 1268 | Plin. 20. 59 | Caper decoction | drink | Toothache |
| 1269 | Plin. 20. 59 | Caper root | masticant | Toothache |
| 1270 | Plin. 20. 59 | Caper boiled in oil (injection) | ear drops | Ear ache |
| 1271 | Plin. 20. 59 | Caper leaves, or fresh root w/ honey | topical | Phagedaenic sores |
| 1272 | Plin. 20. 59 | Fresh root w/ honey | topical | Scrofula |
| 1273 | Plin. 20. 59 | Capers boiled | drink | Parotid tumours and worms |
| 1274 | Plin. 20. 59 | Capers pounded w/ barley meal | topical | Pains in the liver |
| 1275 | Plin. 20. 59 | Capers | | Diseases of bladder |
| 1276 | Plin. 20. 59 | Capers w/ vinegar and honey | drink | Tapeworm |
| 1277 | Plin. 20. 59 | Capper and vinegar decoction | drink | Sores in the mouth |
| 1278 | Plin. 20. 59 | Capers | | Harmful to stomach |
| 1279 | Plin. 20. 60 | Lovage | oral | Good for stomach, convulsions and flatulence |
| 1280 | Plin. 20. 61 | Ox cunila (chewed and applied to wounds (left on for 5 days) | masticant | Heals wounds |

| | | | | |
|---|---|---|---|---|
| 1281 | Plin. 20. 61 | Ox cunila pounded w/ wine | drink | Bites of serpents |
| 1282 | Plin. 20. 61 | Ox cunila dry or after pounding the leaves | topical | Tumours problems with the male organs |
| 1283 | Plin. 20. 61 | Ox cunila w/ wine | drink | Combines well w/ wine all treatments |
| 1284 | Plin. 20. 62 | Chicken cunila w/ salt | | Good for eyes |
| 1285 | Plin. 20. 62 | Chicken cunila w/ meal oil and vinegar | drink | Cough, liver complaints and pains in the side |
| 1286 | Plin. 20. 62 | Chicken cunila w/ meal oil and vinegar | drink | Snake bites |
| 1287 | Plin. 20. 63 | Male cunila (cunilago) w/ vinegar and water | bath | Deters scorpions |
| 1288 | Plin. 20. 63 | Male cunila (3 leaves) w/ oil | bath | Serpents kept away |
| 1289 | Plin. 20. 64 | Soft cunila or libanotis cunila w/ wine or vinegar | oral | Antidote against snake bite |
| 1290 | Plin. 20. 64 | Soft cunila or libanotis cunila w/ water | topical | Kill fleas |
| 1291 | Plin. 20. 65 | Cunila juice w/ rose oil | topical | Ear laps |
| 1292 | Plin. 20. 65 | Cunila juice | drink | Stings |
| 1293 | Plin. 20. 65 | Mountain cunila | topical | Bites of serpents |
| 1294 | Plin. 20. 65 | Mountain cunila | oral | Diuretic and cleanses afterbirth |
| 1295 | Plin. 20. 65 | Cunila | oral | Digestion and appetite |
| 1296 | Plin. 20. 65 | Cunila (while fasting) sprinkled in drink | drink | Indigestion |
| 1297 | Plin. 20. 65 | Cunila | | Sprains |
| 1298 | Plin. 20. 65 | Cunila w/ barley meal, vinegar or water | oral | Stings of wasps and the like |
| 1299 | Plin. 20. 66 | Piperitis w/ drink | drink | Epilepsy |
| 1300 | Plin. 20. 66 | Piperitis | oral | Good for gums, teeth, belching, sweetness of breath |
| 1301 | Plin. 20. 67 | Wild marjoram w/ warm water | drink | Gnawing of the stomach and indigestion |
| 1302 | Plin. 20. 67 | Wild marjoram/ white wine | drink | Stings of spiders and scorpions |
| 1303 | Plin. 20. 67 | Wild marjoram on wool w/ vinegar and oil | topical | Sprains and bruises |
| 1304 | Plin. 20. 68 | Goat oregano | oral | Diuretic disperses tumours |

| | | | | |
|---|---|---|---|---|
| 1305 | Plin. 20. 68 | Goat oregano w/ drink | drink | Mistletoe poisoning, viper bites, acid belching and the hypochondria |
| 1306 | Plin. 20. 68 | Goats oregano w/ honey | oral | Coughs pleurisy and pneumonia |
| 1307 | Plin. 20. 69 | Heraclium | smell | Keep away serpents |
| 1308 | Plin. 20. 69 | Heraclium boiled | oral | Snake bites |
| 1309 | Plin. 20. 69 | Heraclium boiled | drink | Diuretic |
| 1310 | Plin. 20. 69 | Heraclium w/ all heal root | oral | Ruptures and convulsions |
| 1311 | Plin. 20. 69 | Heraclium w/ fig or hyssop boiled to 1/6 (1 acetabulum) | oral | Dropsy |
| 1312 | Plin. 20. 69 | Heraclium w/ fig or hyssop boiled to 1/6 (1 acetabulum) when going to bath | oral | Itch, prurigo and psoriasis |
| 1313 | Plin. 20. 69 | Heraclium juice w/ woman's milk | ear drops | |
| 1314 | Plin. 20. 69 | Heraclium | oral | Tonsils, uvula and sores on the head |
| 1315 | Plin. 20. 69 | Heraclium boiled w/ wine and ashes | drink | Antidote to opium and gypsum |
| 1316 | Plin. 20. 69 | Heraclium (1 acetabulum) | oral | Loosens the bowels |
| 1317 | Plin. 20. 69 | Heraclium | topical | Bruises, and toothache |
| 1318 | Plin. 20. 69 | Heraclium w/ honey and soda | dentifrice | Whitens teeth |
| 1319 | Plin. 20. 69 | Heraclium | topical | Nosebleed |
| 1320 | Plin. 20. 69 | Heraclium boiled w/ barley meal | | Parotid tumours |
| 1321 | Plin. 20. 69 | Heraclium w/ gall nut and honey | oral | Rough trachea |
| 1322 | Plin. 20. 69 | Heraclium leaves w/ honey and salt | oral | Spleen |
| 1323 | Plin. 20. 69 | Heraclium boiled w/ vinegar and salt | oral | Loosens black phlegm |
| 1324 | Plin. 20. 69 | Heraclium beaten w/ oil | nose drops | Jaundice |
| 1325 | Plin. 20. 69 | Heraclium (rubbed w/) | bath | Tired bodies |
| 1326 | Plin. 20. 69 | Heraclium w/ pitch | topical | Epinyctis |
| 1327 | Plin. 20. 69 | Heraclium w/ roasted fig | topical | Boils |
| 1328 | Plin. 20. 69 | Heraclium w/ oil vinegar and barley meal | | Scrofulous swellings |

| | | | | |
|---|---|---|---|---|
| 1329 | Plin. 20. 69 | Heraclium w/ fig | oral | Pains in side |
| 1330 | Plin. 20. 69 | Heraclium pounded w/ vinegar | topical | Fluxes of blood from the genitals |
| 1331 | Plin. 20. 69 | Heraclium pounded w/ vinegar | topical | Bringing away afterbirth |
| 1332 | Plin. 20. 70 | Dittander (pepperwort) | topical | Clears complexion but produces sores |
| 1333 | Plin. 20. 70 | Wax and rose oil | topical | Clear the sores left by dittander |
| 1334 | Plin. 20. 70 | Used as per 1333 and 1334 | topical | Removes leprous sores, psoriasis and sores left by scars |
| 1335 | Plin. 20. 70 | Dittander (attached to arm) | topical | Draws away (to itself) the pain of toothache |
| 1336 | Plin. 20. 71 | Git (roman coriander) w/ vinegar and honey | topical | Cures wounds of scorpion and snake |
| 1337 | Plin. 20. 71 | Git burnt | fumigation | Snakes kept away |
| 1338 | Plin. 20. 71 | Git (1 drachma) in drink | drink | Spider bite |
| 1339 | Plin. 20. 71 | Git pounded in linen | smell | Stops nose running |
| 1340 | Plin. 20. 71 | Git w/ vinegar | smell | Headaches |
| 1341 | Plin. 20. 71 | Git w/ iris juice | nose drops | Fluxes and swelling of the eyes |
| 1342 | Plin. 20. 71 | Git boiled in vinegar | drink | Toothache |
| 1343 | Plin. 20. 71 | Git pounded in linen | masticant | Mouth ulcers |
| 1344 | Plin. 20. 71 | Git w/ vinegar | topical | Leprous sores and freckles |
| 1345 | Plin. 20. 71 | Git w/ drink and soda | drink | Difficulty breathing |
| 1346 | Plin. 20. 71 | Git | liniment | Chronic swellings and suppurations |
| 1347 | Plin. 20. 71 | Git | oral | Increases woman's milk production |
| 1348 | Plin. 20. 71 | Git juice | drink | Poisonous in large doses |
| 1349 | Plin. 20. 71 | Git juice | drink | Cleanses eye, diuretic and emmenagogue |
| 1350 | Plin. 20. 71 | Git (30 grains) tied to body | topical | Afterbirth is brought away |
| 1351 | Plin. 20. 71 | Git pounded w/ urine | topical | Cures corns of the feet |
| 1352 | Plin. 20. 71 | Git | fumigation | Kills gnats and fleas |
| 1353 | Plin. 20. 72 | Anise (raw or boiled) w/ wine | drink | Scorpion stings |

| | | | | |
|---|---|---|---|---|
| 1354 | Plin. 20. 72 | Anise w/ alexanders and a little honey (rinse w/ wine) | masticant | Bad breath |
| 1355 | Plin. 20. 72 | Anise | | Makes the face look younger |
| 1356 | Plin. 20. 72 | Anise (on pillow) | smell | Relieves sleeplessness |
| 1357 | Plin. 20. 72 | Anise | oral | Sharpens appetite |
| 1358 | Plin. 20. 73 | Anise burned and inhaled through nose | fumigation | Headache |
| 1359 | Plin. 20. 73 | Anise root | topical | Eye fluxes |
| 1360 | Plin. 20. 73 | Anise plant w/ saffron and wine | topical | Eye fluxes |
| 1361 | Plin. 20. 73 | Anise w/ pearl barley | topical | Violent fluxes, and extracting things which have got into the eye |
| 1362 | Plin. 20. 73 | Anise w/ water | topical | Cancers in the nose |
| 1363 | Plin. 20. 73 | Anise w/ hyssop and honey in vinegar | gargle | Quinsy |
| 1364 | Plin. 20. 73 | Anise w/ rose oil | ear drops | Ear ailments |
| 1365 | Plin. 20. 73 | Parched anise w/ honey | drink | Phlegm in chest |
| 1366 | Plin. 20. 73 | Bitter almonds peeled (50) and anise (1 acetabulum) w/ honey | oral | Cough |
| 1367 | Plin. 20. 73 | Anise (3 drachmae), poppy seed (2 drachmae) w/ honey divide to bean size 3 doses daily | oral | Cough |
| 1368 | Plin. 20. 73 | Anise | oral | Flatulence of the stomach, gripping the intestines and colic trouble |
| 1369 | Plin. 20. 73 | Anise boiled | drink or smell | Hiccoughs |
| 1370 | Plin. 20. 73 | Anise leaves boiled | oral | Indigestion |
| 1371 | Plin. 20. 73 | Anise juice w/ boiled celery | smell | Stops sneezing |
| 1372 | Plin. 20. 73 | Anise in drink | drink | Promotes sleep |
| 1373 | Plin. 20. 73 | Anise in drink | drink | Disperses stone |
| 1374 | Plin. 20. 73 | Anise in drink | drink | Stops vomiting and swelling of the hypochondria |
| 1375 | Plin. 20. 73 | Anise in drink | drink | Chest troubles |
| 1376 | Plin. 20. 73 | Anise in drink | drink | Sinews |

| | | | | |
|---|---|---|---|---|
| 1377 | Plin. 20. 73 | Anise juice boiled w/ oil | topical | Headache |
| 1378 | Plin. 20. 73 | Anise roasted | oral | Dysentery and tenesmus |
| 1379 | Plin. 20. 73 | Anise w/ opium (pills the size of lupine seed) 3 times a day w/ wine (1 cyathus) | oral | Dysentery and tenesmus |
| 1380 | Plin. 20. 73 | Anise juice | drink | Lumbago |
| 1381 | Plin. 20. 73 | Anise seed pounded w/ mint | oral | Dropsy and coeliac trouble |
| 1382 | Plin. 20. 73 | Anise root | oral | Diseases of the kidneys |
| 1383 | Plin. 20. 73 | Anise and parsley | poultice | Women in labour and pain in the womb |
| 1384 | Plin. 20. 73 | Anise w/ dill in drink | drink | Women in labour |
| 1385 | Plin. 20. 73 | Anise w/ pearl barley | topical | Phrenitis |
| 1386 | Plin. 20. 73 | Anise w/ pearl barley | topical | Babies w/ epilepsy or convulsions |
| 1387 | Plin. 20. 73 | Anise (in hand) | topical/folk | Prevents epileptic fit |
| 1388 | Plin. 20. 73 | Anise | smell | Makes birth easier |
| 1389 | Plin. 20. 73 | Anise w/ pearl barley | drink | To be given after delivery |
| 1390 | Plin. 20. 73 | Anise w/ vinegar | drink | Indurations |
| 1391 | Plin. 20. 73 | Anise w/ soda boiled in oil | | Fatigue |
| 1392 | Plin. 20. 73 | Anise seed in drink | drink | Less fatigue when traveling |
| 1393 | Plin. 20. 73 | Anise seed (3 finger pinch) w/ honey wine and beaver oil(2 oboli) | drink | Flatulence of the stomach, belly and intestines |
| 1394 | Plin. 20. 73 | Anise seed (3 finger pinch), henbane (3 finger pinch) w/ asses milk | drink | Orthopnoea |
| 1395 | Plin. 20. 73 | Water w/ *lacuna* acetabula of anise and 10 pounded bay leaves | drink | Before taking an emetic |
| 1396 | Plin. 20. 73 | Anise chewed and applied warm | topical | Suffocation of the womb |
| 1397 | Plin. 20. 73 | Anise w/ beaver oil and oxymel | drink | Suffocation of the womb |
| 1398 | Plin. 20. 73 | Cucumber seed (3 finger pinch) linseed (3 finger pinch) w/ white wine (3 cyaths) | drink | Dispels vertigo after birth |
| 1399 | Plin. 20. 73 | Anise seed (3 finger pinch) w/ fennel, vinegar and honey (1 cyath) | oral | Quartan agues |
| 1400 | Plin. 20. 73 | Anise w/ bitter almonds | topical | Diseases of the joints |

| | | | | |
|---|---|---|---|---|
| 1401 | Plin. 20. 73 | Anise | | oral | Antidote for asp poison |
| 1402 | Plin. 20. 73 | Anise | | oral | Diuretic, quenches thirst, aphrodisiac |
| 1403 | Plin. 20. 73 | Anise w/ wine | | drink | Promotes a gentle perspiration |
| 1404 | Plin. 20. 73 | Anise | | smell | Protects clothes from moths |
| 1405 | Plin. 20. 73 | Anise | | oral | Injures stomach except when theirs flatulence |
| 1406 | Plin. 20. 74 | Dill | | oral | Causes belching and relives gripping |
| 1407 | Plin. 20. 74 | Dill | | oral | Stops diarrhoea |
| 1408 | Plin. 20. 74 | Dill roots w/ water or wine | | topical | Eye fluxes |
| 1409 | Plin. 20. 74 | Dill seed boiling | | smell | Hiccoughs |
| 1410 | Plin. 20. 74 | Dill w/ water | | drink | Indigestion |
| 1411 | Plin. 20. 74 | Dill ash | | oral | Inflamed uvula but weakens sight and powers of generation |
| 1412 | Plin. 20. 75 | Sagapemon in drink or w/ oil as embrocation | | drink | Pains in the side and chest, convulsions chronic coughs |
| 1413 | Plin. 20. 75 | Sagapemon in drink or w/ oil as embrocation | | drink | Expectoration and inflammation of the hypochondria |
| 1414 | Plin. 20. 75 | Sagapemon in drink or w/ oil as embrocation | | drink | Vertigo, palsy and opisthotonic tetanus |
| 1415 | Plin. 20. 75 | Sagapemon in drink or w/ oil as embrocation | | drink | Diseases of the spleen and loins and violent chills |
| 1416 | Plin. 20. 75 | Sagapemon w/vinegar | | smell | Suffocation of the womb |
| 1417 | Plin. 20. 75 | Sagapemon | | oral | Useful as an antidote to harmful drugs |
| 1418 | Plin. 20. 76 | White poppy calyx w/ wine | | drink | Induce sleep |
| 1419 | Plin. 20. 76 | White poppy seed | | oral | Elephantiasis |
| 1420 | Plin. 20. 76 | Dark poppy resin (soporific) obtained by slicing buds at the third hour of the day incision made beneath the calyx not in the head itself | | | |
| 1421 | Plin. 20. 76 | Resin dried and made into a lozenge (called opium) | | oral | Induces sleep (may cause death) |
| 1422 | Plin. 20. 76 | Poppy juice | | injections | Harmful to eyesight |
| 1423 | Plin. 20. 76 | Poppy seed pounded w/ milk | | drink | Induces sleep |

| ID | Reference | Description | Administration | Use |
|---|---|---|---|---|
| 1424 | Plin. 20. 76 | Poppy seed w/ rose oil | | Headache |
| 1425 | Plin. 20. 76 | Poppy seed w/ rose oil | | Earache |
| 1426 | Plin. 20. 76 | Opium or poppy leaves w/ woman's milk | ear drops | Gout |
| 1427 | Plin. 20. 76 | Opium w/ vinegar | liniment | Erysipelas and wounds |
| 1428 | Plin. 20. 76 | Pliny discouraged opium use for the following | liniment | Eye salves, febrifuges, coeliac and digestives |
| 1429 | Plin. 20. 76 | Dark poppy w/ wine | drink | Coeliac trouble |
| 1430 | Plin. 20. 76 | Poppy boiled (decoction) | drink | Sleeplessness |
| 1431 | Plin. 20. 76 | Poppy boiled (decoction) | fomentation | |
| 1432 | Plin. 20. 76 | Heads and leaves are boiled to make meconium (weaker than opium) | | |
| 1433 | Plin. 20. 76 | How to test opium quality and preserve it | | |
| 1434 | Plin. 20. 77 | Roaming poppy (self-seeded) flower eaten | oral | Purge |
| 1435 | Plin. 20. 77 | 5 heads of roaming poppy boiled in 3 heminae of water | drink | Induce sleep |
| 1436 | Plin. 20. 78 | Ceratitis (wild poppy) (1/2 acetabulum) w/ honey wine | drink | Purge |
| 1437 | Plin. 20. 78 | Ceratitis leaves w/ oil | | Eye ulcers of beasts of burden |
| 1438 | Plin. 20. 78 | Ceratitis root (1 acetabulum) w/ water (2sextarii) boiled to 1/2 | drink | Complaints of loin and liver |
| 1439 | Plin. 20. 78 | Ceratitis leaves w/ honey | topical | Carbuncles |
| 1440 | Plin. 20. 79 | Heraclium (wild poppy) pounded (1 acetabulum) w/ white wine | drink | Epilepsy |
| 1441 | Plin. 20. 79 | Heraclinum | oral | Causes vomiting and is useful for the drug diacodion or aratriace |
| 1442 | Plin. 20. 79 | Diacodion and aratriace = wild poppy heads (120) in rain water (3 sextari) for 2 days then boil mix an dry then boil again on low heat w/ honey | drink | |
| 1443 | Plin. 20. 79 | Newer version of diacodion and aratriace (which Pliny believes is no better) adds saffron, hypocisthis, frankincense and gum of acacia(6 drachmae) w/ Cretian raisin wine (1 sextarius) | drink | |
| 1444 | Plin. 20. 80 | Tithymalon (wild poppy) seed w/ 1/2 acetabulum of honey wine | oral | Purges the bowels |
| 1445 | Plin. 20. 80 | Poppy head fresh or dried | topical | Relieves eye fluxes |

| # | Ref | Preparation | Application | Use |
|---|---|---|---|---|
| 1446 | Plin. 20. 80 | Opium in nearly neat wine | drink | Antidote to scorpion stings |
| 1447 | Plin. 20. 80 | Dark poppy heads or leaves ground w/ wine | drink | Antidote to scorpion stings |
| 1448 | Plin. 20. 81 | Peplis (euphorbia peplis) | oral | Antidote to arrow poison and haemorrhois (snake) bite |
| 1449 | Plin. 20. 81 | Peplis (euphorbia peplis) | topical | Poison is drawn out |
| 1450 | Plin. 20. 81 | Peplis after juice extraction w/ raisin wine | drink | Henbane poison |
| 1451 | Plin. 20. 81 | Seed has similar effect as 1449 -1451 | | Poison |
| 1452 | Plin. 20. 81 | Peplis | drink | Purifies water |
| 1453 | Plin. 20. 81 | Peplis pounded w/ wine | topical | Headache and sores on the head |
| 1454 | Plin. 20. 81 | Peplis chewed w/ honey | topical | Other sores |
| 1455 | Plin. 20. 81 | Peplis chewed w/ honey | topical | Cranium of infants |
| 1456 | Plin. 20. 81 | Peplis chewed w/ honey | topical | Umbilical hernia |
| 1457 | Plin. 20. 81 | Peplis w/ pearl barley on head and temples | topical | Eye fluxes |
| 1458 | Plin. 20. 81 | Peplis w/ milk and honey eyes themselves | topical | Eye fluxes |
| 1459 | Plin. 20. 81 | Pounded peplis leaves w/ bean husks, blisters, pearl barley salt and vinegar | topical | Eyes falling forward |
| 1460 | Plin. 20. 81 | Peplis raw | masticant | Mouth sores and gumboils |
| 1461 | Plin. 20. 81 | Peplis boiled juice w/ myrrh | drink | Toothache and sore tonsils |
| 1462 | Plin. 20. 81 | Peplis | masticant | Makes loose teeth firm, strengthens the voice, keeps away thirst |
| 1463 | Plin. 20. 81 | Peplis w/ gall nut, linseed and honey (equal) | topical | Pains of the back or neck |
| 1464 | Plin. 20. 81 | Peplis w/ honey and Cimolian chalk | topical | Breast complaints |
| 1465 | Plin. 20. 81 | Peplis seed w/ honey | oral | Asthma |
| 1466 | Plin. 20. 81 | Peplis | oral | Strengthens stomach |
| 1467 | Plin. 20. 81 | Peplis w/ pearl barley | topical | High temperature |
| 1468 | Plin. 20. 81 | Peplis | masticant | Cools the intestines |
| 1469 | Plin. 20. 81 | Peplis | oral | Stops vomiting |

| | | | | |
|---|---|---|---|---|
| 1470 | Plin. 20. 81 | Peplis eaten w/ vinegar or in drink w/ cumin | oral, drink | Dysentery and abscesses |
| 1471 | Plin. 20. 81 | Peplis boiled | drink | Tenesmus |
| 1472 | Plin. 20. 81 | Peplis | oral | Epilepsy |
| 1473 | Plin. 20. 81 | Peplis (1 acetabulum) w/ concentrated must | oral | Menstruation |
| 1474 | Plin. 20. 81 | Peplis w/ salt | topical | Hot gout or erysipelas |
| 1475 | Plin. 20. 81 | Peplis juice | drink | Helps kidneys and bladder and expels parasites |
| 1476 | Plin. 20. 81 | Peplis w/ oil and pearl barley | topical | Pain of a wound |
| 1477 | Plin. 20. 81 | Peplis | | Softens indurations of the sinews |
| 1478 | Plin. 20. 81 | Peplis (after delay) | oral | Aid afterbirth |
| 1479 | Plin. 20. 81 | Peplis | oral | Stops lust and amorous dreams |
| 1480 | Plin. 20. 81 | Peplis (worn around neck) | folk topical | Disease of the uvula |
| 1481 | Plin. 20. 81 | Peplis ointment (on head) | topical | Free from catarrh all year |
| 1482 | Plin. 20. 81 | Peplis | | Weakens eyesight |
| 1483 | Plin. 20. 82 | Coriander in drink or applied | drink topical | Antidote to amphisbaena (snake) bite |
| 1484 | Plin. 20. 82 | Coriander pounded | topical | Night rashes and blisters |
| 1485 | Plin. 20. 82 | Coriander pounded | topical | Tumours and gatherings |
| 1486 | Plin. 20. 82 | Coriander pounded w/ vinegar | topical | Panus (superficial abscess to the hear follicle) |
| 1487 | Plin. 20. 82 | Coriander seed (3) | oral | Before fit of tertian ague |
| 1488 | Plin. 20. 82 | Coriander seed (< 3) in ointment on forehead | topical | Before fit of tertian ague |
| 1489 | Plin. 20. 82 | Fresh coriander | topical | Cool inflammations |
| 1490 | Plin. 20. 82 | Coriander w/ honey or raisons | topical | Spreading sores |
| 1491 | Plin. 20. 82 | Coriander w/ honey or raisons | topical | Diseased testis, burns carbuncles and sore ears |
| 1492 | Plin. 20. 82 | Coriander w/ woman's milk | topical | Eye fluxes |
| 1493 | Plin. 20. 82 | Coriander seed w/ water | drink | Fluxes from belly or intestines |
| 1494 | Plin. 20. 82 | Coriander w/ rue in drink | drink | Cholera |
| 1495 | Plin. 20. 82 | Coriander seed w/ pomegranate juice and oil | drink | Intestinal parasites |

| | | | | |
|---|---|---|---|---|
| 1496 | Plin. 20. 82 | Grain of coriander seed in drink | | Delays menses by one day per grain |
| 1497 | Plin. 20. 83 | Orache | drink | May cause dropsy jaundice and pallor hard to digest |
| 1498 | Plin. 20. 83 | Orache | | Nothing can grow near it |
| 1499 | Plin. 20. 83 | Orache | | Causes freckles and pimples |
| 1500 | Plin. 20. 83 | Orache | | If boiled water must be changed often |
| 1501 | Plin. 20. 83 | Orache | | Injures the stomach |
| 1502 | Plin. 20. 83 | Orache w/ beet | injection | Complaints of the womb |
| 1503 | Plin. 20. 83 | Orache w/ drink | drink | Sting of the Spanish fly |
| 1504 | Plin. 20. 83 | Orache raw or boiled | topical | Superficial abscesses, incipient boils and all indurations |
| 1505 | Plin. 20. 83 | Orache w/ honey vinegar and soda | topical | Erysipelas and gout |
| 1506 | Plin. 20. 83 | Orache | topical | Removes scabrous nails without leaving a sore |
| 1507 | Plin. 20. 83 | Orache seed w/ honey | oral | Jaundice |
| 1508 | Plin. 20. 83 | Orache seed w/ honey and soda | bath | Rub throat and tonsils |
| 1509 | Plin. 20. 83 | Orache boiled w/ or without mallows or lentils | oral | Purge |
| 1510 | Plin. 20. 83 | Orache | oral | Emetic |
| 1511 | Plin. 20. 84 | Malache (mallow) | oral | Relaxes the bowels |
| 1512 | Plin. 20. 84 | Mallow | topical | Treat stings (esp. Scorpions, wasps and shrew mouse) |
| 1513 | Plin. 20. 84 | Mallow and oil or mallow carried | bath | Never stung |
| 1514 | Plin. 20. 84 | Mallow | oral | Counteract the poison of white lead |
| 1515 | Plin. 20. 84 | Raw mallow w/ saltpetre | topical | Extracts splinters and thorns |
| 1516 | Plin. 20. 84 | Mallow root boiled (some say you must also induce vomiting) | oral | Counteracts poison of sea hare |
| 1517 | Plin. 20. 84 | Mallow juice (1/2 cyahtus ) | drink | Immune to all diseases |
| 1518 | Plin. 20. 84 | Mallows rotted in urine | topical | Running sores of the head |
| 1519 | Plin. 20. 84 | Mallow and honey | topical, | Lichen and sores in the mouth |

| | | | | | |
|---|---|---|---|---|---|
| 1520 | Plin. 20. 84 | Mallow root decoction | | gargle | Dandruff and loose teeth |
| 1521 | Plin. 20. 84 | Root of single stemmed mallow (stabbed around tooth) | | topical | Toothache |
| 1522 | Plin. 20. 84 | Root or plant (unclear) of single stemmed mallow | | topical | Scrofula and parotid abscesses |
| 1523 | Plin. 20. 84 | Root or plant (unclear) of single stemmed mallow w/ saliva | | topical | Superficial abscesses |
| 1524 | Plin. 20. 84 | Mallow seed in dark wine | | drink | Phlegm and nausea |
| 1525 | Plin. 20. 84 | Mallow root in dark wool as amulet | | folk | Prevent breast problems |
| 1526 | Plin. 20. 84 | Mallow boiled in milk (5 day course) | | drink | Cough |
| 1527 | Plin. 20. 84 | Mallows rotted in urine | | | Injure the stomach |
| 1528 | Plin. 20. 84 | Mallows w/ goose grease | | topical | Cause abortion |
| 1529 | Plin. 20. 84 | Mallow leaves (handful) in oil and wine | | drink | Assist menstruation |
| 1530 | Plin. 20. 84 | Mallow leaves under women in labour | | folk | Deliver more quickly |
| 1531 | Plin. 20. 84 | Mallow juice (hemina) boiled in wine | | drink | Woman in labour |
| 1532 | Plin. 20. 84 | Mallow seed (attached to arms) | | topical | Spermatorrhoea |
| 1533 | Plin. 20. 84 | Mallow seed | | oral | Aphrodisiac |
| 1534 | Plin. 20. 84 | Mallow roots (3) near vagina | | topical | Aphrodisiac |
| 1535 | Plin. 20. 84 | Mallow | | injections or fomentation | Tenesmus, dysentery and rectal troubles |
| 1536 | Plin. 20. 84 | Mallow juice (3 cyathi) | | drink | Melancholia |
| 1537 | Plin. 20. 84 | Mallow juice (4 cyathi) | | drink | Raving |
| 1538 | Plin. 20. 84 | Decocted mallow juice (1 hemina) | | drink | Epilepsy |
| 1539 | Plin. 20. 84 | Mallow juice warm | | drink | Stone, flatulence, gripping and apisthotonus |
| 1540 | Plin. 20. 84 | Mallow leaves boiled to an oily paste | | topical | Erysipelas and burns |
| 1541 | Plin. 20. 84 | Mallow leaves raw w/ bread | | poultice | Painful wounds |
| 1542 | Plin. 20. 84 | Mallow decoction juice | | drink | Sinews, bladder and gnawing of the intestines |
| 1543 | Plin. 20. 84 | Mallow past | | oral, | Soothes the womb |

| | | | | |
|---|---|---|---|---|
| 1544 | Plin. 20. 84 | Althea root | injection | More effective than mallow 1513 - 1544 esp. Spasms and ruptures |
| 1545 | Plin. 20. 84 | Althea root boiled in water | drink | Stops loose bowels |
| 1546 | Plin. 20. 84 | Althea root w/ white wine | drink | Scrofula, parotid abscesses and inflammation of the breast |
| 1547 | Plin. 20. 84 | Althea leaves boiled in wine | topical | Superficial abscesses |
| 1548 | Plin. 20. 84 | Althea leaves dried and boiled in milk | drink | Cough |
| 1549 | Plin. 20. 84 | Althea root boiled down | drink | Thirsty wounded soldiers |
| 1550 | Plin. 20. 84 | Althea w/ honey and resin | topical | Wounds |
| 1551 | Plin. 20. 84 | Althea w/ honey and resin | topical | Bruises sprains and swellings |
| 1552 | Plin. 20. 84 | Althea w/ honey and resin | topical | Muscles sinews and joints |
| 1553 | Plin. 20. 84 | Althea w/ wine | drink | Cramp or dysentery |
| 1554 | Plin. 20. 85 | Wild sorrel root w/ axel grease | topical | Scrofula |
| 1555 | Plin. 20. 85 | Wild sorrel | topical | Heal the wounds of scorpions and prevent bite when carried |
| 1556 | Plin. 20. 85 | Sorrel root boiled in vinegar | mouthwash | Good for teeth |
| 1557 | Plin. 20. 85 | Sorrel root boiled in vinegar | drink | Jaundice |
| 1558 | Plin. 20. 85 | Sorrel seed | oral | Inveterate stomach troubles |
| 1559 | Plin. 20. 85 | Root of horse sorrel | topical | Scabrous nails |
| 1560 | Plin. 20. 85 | Sorrel seed (2 drachmae) w/ wine | drink | Dysentery |
| 1561 | Plin. 20. 85 | Pointed sorrel seed washed in rain water w/ gum acacia (lentil size) | oral | Spitting of blood |
| 1562 | Plin. 20. 85 | Sorrel leaves and root w/ soda and a little frankincense (to use steep lozenge in vinegar) | lozenge | |
| 1563 | Plin. 20. 86 | Cultivated sorrel on forehead | topical | Eye fluxes |
| 1564 | Plin. 20. 86 | Sorrel root | topical | Lichen and leprous sores |
| 1565 | Plin. 20. 86 | Sorrel boiled in wine | drink | Scrofula and parotid abscesses |

| | | | | |
|---|---|---|---|---|
| 1566 | Plin. 20. 86 | Sorrel w/ wine | drink | Stone |
| 1567 | Plin. 20. 86 | Sorrel | liniment | Spleen and coeliac troubles dysentery and tessimus |
| 1568 | Plin. 20. 86 | Sorrel | | Causes belching, is diuretic, removes dimness of sight |
| 1569 | Plin. 20. 86 | Sorrel rubbed on body | bath | Stops bodily itching |
| 1570 | Plin. 20. 86 | Sorrel put in the bottom of a bath | bath | Stops bodily itching |
| 1571 | Plin. 20. 86 | Sorrel root | masticant | Strengthens loose teeth |
| 1572 | Plin. 20. 86 | Sorrel decoction w/ wine | drink | Checks looseness of the bowels |
| 1573 | Plin. 20. 86 | Sorrel leaves decoction | drink | Relax bowels |
| 1574 | Plin. 20. 86 | Ox sorrel root | oral | Dysentery |
| 1575 | Plin. 20. 87 | Mustard pounded w/ vinegar | topical | Serpent and scorpion stings |
| 1576 | Plin. 20. 87 | Mustard pounded w/ vinegar | oral | Poisons of fungi |
| 1577 | Plin. 20. 87 | Mustard kept in mouth or used as a gargle w/ hydromel | masticant | Phlegm |
| 1578 | Plin. 20. 87 | Mustard | masticant | Toothache |
| 1579 | Plin. 20. 87 | Mustard w/ vinegar and honey | gargle | Uvula |
| 1580 | Plin. 20. 87 | Mustard | oral | Beneficial to stomach troubles |
| 1581 | Plin. 20. 87 | Mustard w/ food w/ juice of cucumber | oral | Causes expectoration from the lungs for asthmatics and epileptic exhaustion |
| 1582 | Plin. 20. 87 | Mustard | oral | Clears the senses and head |
| 1583 | Plin. 20. 87 | Mustard | oral | Relaxes the bowels causes menstruation and urine |
| 1584 | Plin. 20. 87 | Mustard w/ figs and cumin (equal) | topical | Dropsy |
| 1585 | Plin. 20. 87 | Mustard w/ vinegar | smell | Revives fainted women w/ prolapses, lethargies and epileptics |
| 1586 | Plin. 20. 87 | Mustard w/ heartwort (if severe w/ fig and vinegar) to legs or even head | topical | Lethargies |
| 1587 | Plin. 20. 87 | Mustard w/ fig (applied externally to cause blisters) | topical | Chronic pains in chest, loins hips and shoulders |

134

| | | | | |
|---|---|---|---|---|
| 1588 | Plin. 20. 87 | Mustard w/ red earth | topical | Itch, leprous sores, psoriasis, tetanus and opisthotonos |
| 1589 | Plin. 20. 87 | Mustard w/ honey | topical | Scabrous checks dimness of vision |
| 1590 | Plin. 20. 87 | Mustard juice dried from stem | topical | Cures toothache |
| 1591 | Plin. 20. 87 | Mustard seed and root w/ must | oral | Strengthens throat, stomach, eyes, head and senses |
| 1592 | Plin. 20. 87 | Mustard seed and root w/ must | oral | Lassitude of women |
| 1593 | Plin. 20. 87 | Mustard w/ vinegar | drink | Disperses stone |
| 1594 | Plin. 20. 87 | Mustard w/ honey and goose grease or Cyprian wax | topical | Livid marks and bruises |
| 1595 | Plin. 20. 87 | Mustard seed soaked in oil and pressed (to extract oil) | topical | Stiff sinews, loins and hips and violent chills |
| 1596 | Plin. 20. 89 | Horehound leaves and seeds | topical | Serpent bites, pains in chest and sides and chronic cough |
| 1597 | Plin. 20. 89 | Horehound stalks boiled w/ Italian millet to dilute | drink | Spitting of blood |
| 1598 | Plin. 20. 89 | Horehound w/ grease | topical | Scrofula |
| 1599 | Plin. 20. 89 | Fresh horehound seed (2 finger pinch) w/ emmer (handful) w/ oil and salt | oral | Cough |
| 1600 | Plin. 20. 89 | Horehound and fennel boiled from 3 - 2 sextari then add 1 sextari of honey and boil to 2 dose 1 spoonful w/ cyathus of water | drink | Cough |
| 1601 | Plin. 20. 89 | Horehound w/ honey | topical | Illnesses of the male genitals |
| 1602 | Plin. 20. 89 | Horehound w/ vinegar | | Lichen |
| 1603 | Plin. 20. 89 | Horehound | topical | Ruptures, spasms, cramps and sinews |
| 1604 | Plin. 20. 89 | Horehound w/ salt and vinegar | oral | Relax bowels and aid menstruation and the afterbirth |
| 1605 | Plin. 20. 89 | Horehound dried w/ honey | oral | Dry cough |
| 1606 | Plin. 20. 89 | Horehound dried w/ honey | oral | Gangrene and hangnails |
| 1607 | Plin. 20. 89 | Horehound juice | topical | Ear laps, nostrils, jaundice and lessening bile secretion |
| 1608 | Plin. 20. 89 | Horehound | oral | Antidote to poisons |

| | | | | | |
|---|---|---|---|---|---|
| 1609 | Plin. 20. 89 | Horehound plant w/ iris and honey | | oral | Purges the stomach |
| 1610 | Plin. 20. 89 | Horehound plant w/ iris and honey | | oral | Clears phlegm from lungs, |
| 1611 | Plin. 20. 89 | Horehound plant w/ iris and honey | | oral | Promotes urine avoid if bladder is ulcerated or kidneys effected |
| 1612 | Plin. 20. 89 | Horehound juice | | drink | Improves eyesight |
| 1613 | Plin. 20. 89 | Horehound juice egg and honey | | topical | Abscesses |
| 1614 | Plin. 20. 89 | Pounded horehound w/ old axle grease | | topical | Dog bites |
| 1615 | Plin. 20. 90 | Wild thyme boiled in wine | | drink | Snake bites (esp. Cenchris, scolopendras and scorpions) |
| 1616 | Plin. 20. 90 | Wild thyme burnet | | fumigation | Deters poisonous creatures |
| 1617 | Plin. 20. 90 | Wild thyme | | | Antidote to marine creatures |
| 1618 | Plin. 20. 90 | Wild thyme w/ vinegar and rose oil (on temples and forehead) | | topical | Headache |
| 1619 | Plin. 20. 90 | Wild thyme w/ vinegar and rose oil (on temples and forehead) | | topical | Phrenitis and lethargies |
| 1620 | Plin. 20. 90 | Wild thyme (4 drachmae) w/ water | | drink | Griping, strangury, quinsy and vomiting |
| 1621 | Plin. 20. 90 | Wild thyme leaves (4 oboli) | | oral | Liver complaints |
| 1622 | Plin. 20. 90 | Wild thyme leaves (4 oboli) w/ vinegar | | drink | Spleen troubles |
| 1623 | Plin. 20. 90 | Wild thyme w/ oxymel (2 cyathi) | | drink | Spitting blood |
| 1624 | Plin. 20. 91 | Sisymbruim | | topical | Stings of hornet like creatures |
| 1625 | Plin. 20. 91 | Sisymbruim w/ bread of in wine alone | | topical | Headache and eye fluxes |
| 1626 | Plin. 20. 91 | Sisymbrium | | topical | Heals night rashes and spots on a woman face (in four days) |
| 1627 | Plin. 20. 91 | Sisymbrium (food) or as juice | | oral | Vomiting, coughing, griping and fluxes of the stomach |
| 1628 | Plin. 20. 91 | Sisybrium eaten or topical | | oral topical | Causes abortion |
| 1629 | Plin. 20. 91 | Sisymbrium w/ wine | | drink | Diuretic |
| 1630 | Plin. 20. 91 | Wild sisymbrium (w/ wine?) | | drink? | Expels stone |
| 1631 | Plin. 20. 91 | Sisymbrium w/ vinegar (poured on head) | | topical | Remain awake and keep roused |

| | | | | | |
|---|---|---|---|---|---|
| 1632 | Plin. 20. 92 | Linseed | | topical | Removes spots on a woman's face |
| 1633 | Plin. 20. 92 | Linseed juice | | topical | Improves eyesight |
| 1634 | Plin. 20. 92 | Linseed w/ frankincense and water or myrrh and wine | | | Eye fluxes |
| 1635 | Plin. 20. 92 | Linseed w/ honey or grease or wax | | topical | Parotid abscesses |
| 1636 | Plin. 20. 92 | Linseed w/ water | | drink | Fluxes from the stomach |
| 1637 | Plin. 20. 92 | Linseed boiled in water and oil w/ anise | | topical | Quinsies |
| 1638 | Plin. 20. 92 | Linseed roasted | | oral | Looseness of bowels |
| 1639 | Plin. 20. 92 | Linseed w/ vinegar | | drink | Coeliac troubles and dysentery |
| 1640 | Plin. 20. 92 | Linseed w/ raisins | | oral | Pains of the liver |
| 1641 | Plin. 20. 92 | Linseed seed | | electuaries | Consumption |
| 1642 | Plin. 20. 92 | Linseed meal w/ soda, salt or ash | | oral | Softens indurations of the sinews, muscles joints and nape of neck |
| 1643 | Plin. 20. 92 | Linseed meal w/ soda, salt or ash | | oral | Softens membrane of brain |
| 1644 | Plin. 20. 92 | Linseed w/ fig | | oral | Parotid abscess |
| 1645 | Plin. 20. 92 | Linseed w/ wild cucumber root | | topical | Extracts things piercing the flesh including broken bones |
| 1646 | Plin. 20. 92 | Linseed boiled in wine | | oral | Stops sore from spreading |
| 1647 | Plin. 20. 92 | Linseed w /honey | | oral | Stops eruptions of phlegm |
| 1648 | Plin. 20. 92 | Linseed w/ cress (equal) | | oral | Scabrous nails |
| 1649 | Plin. 20. 92 | Linseed w/ resin and myrrh | | oral | Testis and hernia |
| 1650 | Plin. 20. 92 | Linseed w/ water | | drink | Gangrene |
| 1651 | Plin. 20. 92 | Linseed oil (1 sextarius) w/ fenugreek (equal) in hydromel | | drink | Stomach ache |
| 1652 | Plin. 20. 92 | Linseed in oil or honey | | enema | Dangerous maladies of intestine and lower trunk |
| 1653 | Plin. 20. 93 | False spinach | | oral | Injures stomach |
| 1654 | Plin. 20. 93 | False spinach | | oral | Disturbs bowels to cause cholera |
| 1655 | Plin. 20. 93 | False spinach w/ wine | | drink | Scorpion stings |

| | | | | | |
|---|---|---|---|---|---|
| 1656 | Plin. 20. 93 | False spinach | | liniment | Corns on feet |
| 1657 | Plin. 20. 93 | False spinach w/ oil | | oral | Spleen and pains in temples |
| 1658 | Plin. 20. 93 | False spinach | | oral | Stops menstruation |
| 1659 | Plin. 20. 94 | Spignel root w/ water | | drink | Diuretic, disperses flatulence of stomach |
| 1660 | Plin. 20. 94 | Spignel root w/ water | | drink | Griping troubles of bladder and womb |
| 1661 | Plin. 20. 94 | Spignel w/ honey | | topical | Joints |
| 1662 | Plin. 20. 94 | Spignel w/ celery (on lower abdomen) | | topical | Diuretic for babies |
| 1663 | Plin. 20. 95 | Fennel juice collected when stem is swelling to bud, dried and applied in honey | | ointment | Dimness of vision |
| 1664 | Plin. 20. 95 | Fennel seed | | topical ointment | Dimness of vision |
| 1665 | Plin. 20. 95 | Fennel juice from root when germination has begun | | topical ointment | Dimness of vision |
| 1666 | Plin. 20. 96 | Fennel seeds w/ wine | | drink | Wounds of serpents and scorpions |
| 1667 | Plin. 20. 96 | Fennel juice | | ear drops | Kills ear worms |
| 1668 | Plin. 20. 96 | Fennel plant | | oral | Digestives |
| 1669 | Plin. 20. 96 | Fennel seed | | oral | Tightens relaxed stomach |
| 1670 | Plin. 20. 96 | Fennel pounded w/ water | | oral | Relieves nausea |
| 1671 | Plin. 20. 96 | Fennel | | oral | Complaints of lungs and liver |
| 1672 | Plin. 20. 96 | Fennel (moderate amount) | | oral | Stops looseness of the bowels |
| 1673 | Plin. 20. 96 | Fennel | | oral | Diuretic |
| 1674 | Plin. 20. 96 | Fennel | | decoction | Restores milk to breasts |
| 1675 | Plin. 20. 96 | Fennel root w/ barley water or fennel root juice w/ wine | | drink | Cleanse the kidneys |
| 1676 | Plin. 20. 96 | Fennel root w/ wine | | drink | Dropsy and spasms |
| 1677 | Plin. 20. 96 | Fennel leaves w/ vinegar | | topical | Inflamed tumours |
| 1678 | Plin. 20. 96 | Fennel leaves | | oral | Expel bladder stones |
| 1679 | Plin. 20. 96 | Fennel in all forms | | topical | Creates an abundance of seed (improved fertility) |

| | | | | | |
|---|---|---|---|---|---|
| 1680 | Plin. 20. 96 | Fennel w/ wax | | topical | Bruises |
| 1681 | Plin. 20. 96 | Fennel root in juice or honey | | | Dog bites |
| 1682 | Plin. 20. 96 | Fennel w/ wine | | drink | Multipede sting |
| 1683 | Plin. 20. 96 | Hippomarathum (wild fennel) | | oral | Expels stone well |
| 1684 | Plin. 20. 96 | Hippomarathum (wild fennel) (2 finger pinch) w/ soft wine (seed better than root) | | drink | Bladder and retarded menstruation |
| 1685 | Plin. 20. 96 | Hippomarathum | | | Serpent bites |
| 1686 | Plin. 20. 97 | Hemp seeds | | oral | Make genitals impotent |
| 1687 | Plin. 20. 97 | Hemp juice | | ear drops | Drives out parasites but causes headache |
| 1688 | Plin. 20. 97 | Hemp juice | | drink | Veterinary uses |
| 1689 | Plin. 20. 97 | Hemp root boiled | | drink | Cramped joints, gout and violent pains |
| 1690 | Plin. 20. 97 | Hemp raw | | topical | Burns |
| 1691 | Plin. 20. 98 | Giant fennel stems boiled w/ brine and honey | | oral | Good for stomach (causes headache if too many eaten) |
| 1692 | Plin. 20. 98 | Giant fennel root (1 denarus) w/ wine (2 cyathi) | | drink | Snake bites |
| 1693 | Plin. 20. 98 | Giant fennel root | | topical | Snake bites |
| 1694 | Plin. 20. 98 | Giant fennel root (1 denarus) w/ wine (2 cyathi) | | drink | Griping |
| 1695 | Plin. 20. 98 | Giant fennel in oil and vinegar | | drink | Profuse perspiration even fevers |
| 1696 | Plin. 20. 98 | Giant fennel juice (bean size) | | drink | Loosens bowels |
| 1697 | Plin. 20. 98 | Giant fennel pith | | oral | Good for womb |
| 1698 | Plin. 20. 98 | Giant fennel seeds (10) w/ wine and pith | | oral | Stop bleeding |
| 1699 | Plin. 20. 98 | Giant fennel seed (1 spoonful) from fourth day of the moon to the seventh | | oral | Epilepsy |
| 1700 | Plin. 20. 98 | Juice of the root | | drink | Beneficial to eyesight |
| 1701 | Plin. 20. 99 | Σκόλθμς thistle juice | | topical | Restores skin and hear lost by mange |
| 1702 | Plin. 20. 99 | Thistle root boiled | | drink | Causes thirst in those who are drunkards |
| 1703 | Plin. 20. 99 | Thistle | | oral | Strengthens the stomach |

| | | | | |
|---|---|---|---|---|
| 1704 | Plin. 20. 99 | Thistle | oral | Generates only male children |
| 1705 | Plin. 20. 99 | Thistle gum | lozenge | Makes breath sweet |
| 1706 | Plin. 20. 100 | Wild thyme (2 denarii) opopanax (eq.), spignel (eq.)trefoil seed (1 denarus) aniseed (6 denarii) fennel seed (eq.) ami (eq.) and Parsley (eq.) and (12 denarii) vetch meal; sieve and kneed w/ wine; form lozenges of 1 victoriatus take w/ 3 cyathii of wine | lozenge | Counteract poisons of venomous animals |
| 1707 | Dios. 1. 1. 2 | (African) iris germanicis | oral | Cough |
| 1708 | Dios. 1. 1. 2 | Iris root (7 drachmai) w/ hydromel | drink | Purge thick humours and |
| 1709 | Dios. 1. 1. 2 | Iris root | oral | Induce sleep, cause crying, colic |
| 1710 | Dios. 1. 1. 2 | Iris w/ vinegar | drink | Help those bitten, splenetics, people who have spasms |
| 1711 | Dios. 1. 1. 2 | Iris w/ vinegar | drink | Hypothermics or shiverers, premeture ejaculation |
| 1712 | Dios. 1. 1. 2 | Iris w/ wine | drink | Draws down menses |
| 1713 | Dios. 1. 1. 2 | Iris decoction | vapour Bath | Women's vapour bath |
| 1714 | Dios. 1. 1. 2 | Iris decoction | vapour Bath | Soothing and dilating the genitalia |
| 1715 | Dios. 1. 1. 2 | Iris decoction | clyster | Hip disease |
| 1716 | Dios. 1. 1. 2 | Iris decoction | clyster | Fleshes up ducts and hollows |
| 1717 | Dios. 1. 1. 3 | Iris roots w/ honey | v. sup. | Draw out foetus |
| 1718 | Dios. 1. 1. 3 | Iris roots boiled | cataplasm | Soften scrofulous glands swellings and old indurations |
| 1719 | Dios. 1. 1. 3 | Iris dried and cleanse (ulcers) w/ honey | topical | Fill ulcers |
| 1720 | Dios. 1. 1. 3 | Iris dried | topical | Flesh up bones stripped of flesh |
| 1721 | Dios. 1. 1. 3 | Iris w/ vinegar and unguent roses | plaster | Headaches |
| 1722 | Dios. 1. 1. 3 | Iris w/ vinegar and unguent roses and twice the amount of white hellebore | plaster | Clear birthmarks and freckles |
| 1723 | Dios. 1. 2. 2. | Yellow flag (Iris pseudacorus) decoction | drink | Diuretic pains in side, chest and liver |
| 1724 | Dios. 1. 2. 2. | Yellow flag (Iris pseudacorus) decoction | drink | Colic, ruptures, spasms and reduces the spleen |

| | | | | |
|---|---|---|---|---|
| 1725 | Dios. 1. 2. 2. | Yellow flag (Iris pseudacorus) decoction | drink | Strangury bitten by animals |
| 1726 | Dios. 1. 2. 2. | Yellow flag (Iris pseudacorus) decoction | sitz baths | Woman's complaints |
| 1727 | Dios. 1. 2. 2. | Yellow flag (Iris pseudacorus) root juice | topical | Remove cataracts |
| 1728 | Dios. 1. 3. 1. | Athamantic spignel boiled or ground | drink | Dry bladder and kidneys |
| 1729 | Dios. 1. 3. 1. | Athamantic spignel boiled or ground | drink | Difficult urination, stomach flatulence, colic |
| 1730 | Dios. 1. 3. 1. | Athamantic spignel boiled or ground | drink | Uterine conditions and joint pains |
| 1731 | Dios. 1. 3. 1. | Athamantic spignel ground w/ honey | oral | Chest rheums |
| 1732 | Dios. 1. 3. 1. | Athamantic spignel boiled | sitz bath | Encourage menstruation |
| 1733 | Dios. 1. 3. 1. | Athamantic spignel | plaster | Cause urination |
| 1734 | Dios. 1. 3. 1. | Athamantic spignel (in excess) | drink | Causes headaches |
| 1735 | Dios. 1. 4. 2. | Galingale | drink | Diuretic: kidney stones and edemata |
| 1736 | Dios. 1. 4. 2. | Galingale | | Scorpion sting |
| 1737 | Dios. 1. 4. 2. | Galingale | sitz baths | Uterus chills and closings, aids menstruation |
| 1738 | Dios. 1. 4. 2. | Galingale ground | oral | Mouth sores and spreading ulcers |
| 1739 | Dios. 1. 4. 2. | Galingale w/ heat producing emollients and in thickening unguents | | |
| 1740 | Dios. 1. 5. 1. | Indian' galingale | depilatory | Hair removal |
| 1741 | Dios. 1. 6. 1. | Cardamom w/ water | drink | Epileptics, coughs and patients suffering from hip disease |
| 1742 | Dios. 1. 6. 1. | Cardamom w/ water | drink | Paralysis, ruptures, spasms colic and intestinal flatworm |
| 1743 | Dios. 1. 6. 1. | Cardamom w/ wine | drink | Kidney problems, difficult urination, scorpion stings and animal venoms |
| 1744 | Dios. 1. 6. 1. | Cardamom (1 drachma) w/ bark of sweet bay root | drink | Breaks stones |
| 1745 | Dios. 1. 6. 1. | Cardamom | fumigation | Abortion |
| 1746 | Dios. 1. 6. 1. | Cardamom w/ vinegar | topical | Mange |
| 1747 | Dios. 1. 7. 3. | Spikenard (soaked) oft. Adulterated by powdered antimony (to be removed) | drink | Bind bowel |

| | | | | |
|---|---|---|---|---|
| 1748 | Dios. 1. 7. 3. | Spikenard | v. sup. | Stop uterine bleeding and heavy discharges |
| 1749 | Dios. 1. 7. 4. | Spikenard w/ cold water | drink | Nausea heartburn, flatulence, liver ailments, jaundice and renal dysfunction |
| 1750 | Dios. 1. 7. 4. | Spikenard boiled | sitz bath | Uterine inflammation |
| 1751 | Dios. 1. 7. 4. | Spikenard | topical | Purulent blepharitis |
| 1752 | Dios. 1. 7. 4. | Spikenard | topical | Toning eyelids and increasing eyelash growth |
| 1753 | Dios. 1. 7. 4. | Spikenard powder | topical | Used as a deodorant |
| 1754 | Dios. 1. 7. 4. | Spikenard triturated w/ wine | topical | Eye medication |
| 1755 | Dios. 1. 8. 2. | Celtic spikenard oft. Adulterated by he-goat | | |
| 1756 | Dios. 1. 8. 3. | Celtic spikenard | | Same as Syrian spikenard |
| 1757 | Dios. 1. 8. 3. | Celtic spikenard | oral | More diuretic better for stomach (than Syrian) |
| 1758 | Dios. 1. 8. 3. | Celtic spikenard | oral | Liver inflammations, jaundice |
| 1759 | Dios. 1. 8. 3. | Celtic spikenard w/ wormwood | drink | Flatulence of the stomach |
| 1760 | Dios. 1. 8. 3. | Celtic spikenard | oral | Spleen, kidneys and bladder |
| 1761 | Dios. 1. 8. 3. | Celtic spikenard w/ wine | drink | Venomous bites |
| 1762 | Dios. 1. 8. 3. | Celtic spikenard | | Emollients draughts and warming salves |
| 1763 | Dios. 1. 9. 1. | Same as Celtic spikenard | oral | |
| 1764 | Dios. 1. 10. 1. | Hazelwort | oral | Diuretic warming: edemata and chronic hip disease |
| 1765 | Dios. 1. 10. 1. | Hazelwort | oral | Bring about menses |
| 1766 | Dios. 1. 10. 1. | Hazelwort (7 oungiai) w/ hydromel | drink | Purge (up) |
| 1767 | Dios. 1. 11. 2. | Cretan spikenard decoction | drink | Warm current urination |
| 1768 | Dios. 1. 11. 2. | Cretan spikenard | drink | Warm current urination and pain in side |
| 1769 | Dios. 1. 11. 2. | Cretan spikenard | oral | Bring about menses, mixed with antidotes |
| 1770 | Dios. 1. 11. 2. | Cretan spikenard often adulterated w/ butchers broom | | |
| 1771 | Dios. 1. 12. 2 | Malabar | | Same as spikenard |

| | | | | |
|---|---|---|---|---|
| 1772 | Dios. 1. 12. 2 | Malabar | oral | More diuretic |
| 1773 | Dios. 1. 12. 2 | Malabar | oral | More wholesome |
| 1774 | Dios. 1. 12. 2 | Malabar boiled dried and ground | plaster | Eye inflammations |
| 1775 | Dios. 1. 12. 2 | Malabar placed under tongue | oral | Mouthwash |
| 1776 | Dios. 1. 13. 3. | Cassia | oral | Warming diuretic, desiccative and mildly astringent |
| 1777 | Dios. 1. 13. 3. | Cassia | topical | Short sighted eye medicines and emollients |
| 1778 | Dios. 1. 13. 3. | Cassia w/ honey | topical | Removes birthmarks |
| 1779 | Dios. 1. 13. 3. | Cassia | drink | Brings menses helps bite victims |
| 1780 | Dios. 1. 13. 3. | Cassia | drink | Internal inflammations and kidneys |
| 1781 | Dios. 1. 13. 3. | Cassia (sitz bath or to make thick smoke) | sitz bath or fumigation | Dilating the cervix |
| 1782 | Dios. 1. 13. 3. | Cassia (non-cinnamon) w/ reagents | | Same effect as cinnamon cassia |
| 1783 | Dios. 1. 14. 4. | Cinnamon | oral | Warming, diuretic, emollient and digestive |
| 1784 | Dios. 1. 14. 4. | Cinnamon w/ myrrh | drink | Draw menses and embryo's (abortive) |
| 1785 | Dios. 1. 14. 4. | Cinnamon | oral | Antidote to animal venoms and poisons |
| 1786 | Dios. 1. 14. 4. | Cinnamon | | Clears cataracts |
| 1787 | Dios. 1. 14. 4. | Cinnamon w/ honey | topical | Birthmarks and freckles |
| 1788 | Dios. 1. 14. 4. | Cinnamon | oral | Coughs, head colds, edemata kidney diseases and difficult urination |
| 1789 | Dios. 1. 15. 2. | Nepal cardamom | oral | Warming astringent, desiccative, and soporific |
| 1790 | Dios. 1. 15. 2. | Nepal cardamom on forehead | poultice | Analgesic |
| 1791 | Dios. 1. 15. 2. | Nepal cardamom | topical | Softens and removes boils |
| 1792 | Dios. 1. 15. 2. | Nepal cardamom w/ basil | cataplasm | Scorpion bites |
| 1793 | Dios. 1. 15. 2. | Nepal cardamom | topical | Soothes eye inflammations |
| 1794 | Dios. 1. 15. 2. | Nepal cardamom w/ raisins | oral | Inflammations of internal organs |
| 1795 | Dios. 1. 15. 2. | Nepal cardamom | v. sup.and | Female disorders |

| | | | | |
|---|---|---|---|---|
| 1796 | Dios. 1. 15. 2. | Nepal cardamom decoction | sitz baths | Liver and kidney diseases and gout |
| 1797 | Dios. 1. 15. 2. | Nepal cardamom adulterated by amomis | drink | |
| 1798 | Dios. 1. 16. 1. | Costusroot | | Warm diuretic, emmenagogic |
| 1799 | Dios. 1. 16. 1. | Costusroot | v. sup. | Uterine problems |
| 1800 | Dios. 1. 16. 1. | Costusroot | sitz baths | Uterine problems |
| 1801 | Dios. 1. 16. 1. | Costusroot | anal suppository | Uterine problems |
| 1802 | Dios. 1. 16. 2. | Costusroot (2 oungiai) | drink | Viper bite |
| 1803 | Dios. 1. 16. 2. | Costusroot w/ wormwood, and wine | drink | Chest pains spasms and flatulence |
| 1804 | Dios. 1. 16. 2. | Costusroot w/ honey | drink | Aphrodisiac |
| 1805 | Dios. 1. 16. 2. | Costusroot w/ water | drink | Intestinal flatworms |
| 1806 | Dios. 1. 16. 2. | Costusroot w/ oil | ointment | Shiver (prior to fit) and paralytics |
| 1807 | Dios. 1. 16. 2. | Costusroot w/ water or honey | topical | Removes freckles |
| 1808 | Dios. 1. 16. 2. | Costusroot adulterate w/ commagene calamint | | |
| 1809 | Dios. 1. 17. 2. | Camel hay | | Warm, crush stones, aid digestion, soften open up |
| 1810 | Dios. 1. 17. 2. | Camel hay | | Diuretic, emmenagogic, relax breathing, cause headaches and bind |
| 1811 | Dios. 1. 17. 2. | Camel hay flower | drink | Spitting blood, pains in stomach, lungs, liver, and kidneys |
| 1812 | Dios. 1. 17. 2. | Camel hay root (1 drachma) w/ pepper(eq.) | oral | Nauseous stomachs, edemata and spasms |
| 1813 | Dios. 1. 17. 2. | Camel hay decoction | sitz baths | Uterine inflammation |
| 1814 | Dios. 1. 18. 1. | Sweet flag | masticant | Causes urination |
| 1815 | Dios. 1. 18. 1. | Sweet flag boiled w/ dogtooth grass or celery seed | drink | Edemata, kidney disease, strangury and ruptures |
| 1816 | Dios. 1. 18. 1. | Sweet flag | drink of topical | Causes menstruation |

144

| | | | | |
|---|---|---|---|---|
| 1817 | Dios. 1. 18. 1. | Sweet flag w/ turpentine (burned with smoke inhaled through a tube) | fumigation | Coughs |
| 1818 | Dios. 1. 18. 1. | Sweet flag boiled | sitz baths | |
| 1819 | Dios. 1. 19. 1. | Opobalsamon extracted from mecca balsam by burning rods only 6-7 choes PA | | |
| 1820 | Dios. 1. 19. 2. | Opobalsamon adulterated w/ terebinth, flower of henna, mastic, lilies and metopoion etc. | | |
| 1821 | Dios. 1. 19. 4. | Mecca balsam juice | | Clears cataracts |
| 1822 | Dios. 1. 19. 4. | Mecca balsam w/ cerate of roses | topical | Uterine chills |
| 1823 | Dios. 1. 19. 4. | Mecca balsam | topical | Draws out afterbirth or foetus |
| 1824 | Dios. 1. 19. 4. | Mecca balsam | topical (liniment) | Stops shivering fits |
| 1825 | Dios. 1. 19. 4. | Mecca balsam | topical | Cleanses sores |
| 1826 | Dios. 1. 19. 4. | Mecca balsam | drink | Digestive and diuretic |
| 1827 | Dios. 1. 19. 4. | Mecca balsam | drink | Dyspnea |
| 1828 | Dios. 1. 19. 4. | Mecca balsam | drink | Antidote to leopards bane and milk |
| 1829 | Dios. 1. 19. 4. | Mecca balsam | drink | Bitten by wild animals |
| 1830 | Dios. 1. 19. 5. | Mecca balsam fruit | drink | Pleuristy, lung inflammations, coughs hip diseases |
| 1831 | Dios. 1. 19. 5. | Mecca balsam fruit | drink | Epileptics, dizziness, orthopnea, colic, difficult urination |
| 1832 | Dios. 1. 19. 5. | Mecca balsam fruit | drink | Wild animal bites |
| 1833 | Dios. 1. 19. 5. | Mecca balsam fruit | fumigation | Female diseases (burned bellow) |
| 1834 | Dios. 1. 19. 5. | Mecca balsam fruit boiled down | sitz bath | Dilating the cervix |
| 1835 | Dios. 1. 19. 5. | Mecca balsam wood boiled | drink | Indigestion, colic, venomous bites, spasms and diuretic |
| 1836 | Dios. 1. 19. 5. | Mecca balsam wood boiled w/ iris dried | drink | Head injuries |
| 1837 | Dios. 1. 19. 5. | Mecca balsam | drink | Reduces epithelial waste |

| # | Reference | Substance | Administration | Effect |
|---|---|---|---|---|
| 1838 | Dios. 1. 20. 1. | Camels thorn | | Warming astringent |
| 1839 | Dios. 1. 20. 1. | Camels thorn boiled w/ wine | drink | Mouthwash |
| 1840 | Dios. 1. 20. 1. | Camels thorn | | Thrush |
| 1841 | Dios. 1. 20. 1. | Camels thorn decoction | topical, bath | Filth around genitalia |
| 1842 | Dios. 1. 20. 1. | Camels thorn decoction | topical, bath | Spreading ulcers |
| 1843 | Dios. 1. 20. 1. | Camels thorn decoction | topical, bath | Feted nose sores |
| 1844 | Dios. 1. 20. 1. | Camels thorn | v. sup. | Draws out embryo/foetus |
| 1845 | Dios. 1. 20. 1. | Camels thorn decoction | drink | Stays bowels and spitting blood |
| 1846 | Dios. 1. 20. 1. | Camels thorn decoction | drink | Stops difficult urination and flatulence |
| 1847 | Dios. 1. 21. 1. | Tree moss (from cedar, white poplar and oak) | sitz bath | Astringent: uterine diseases |
| 1848 | Dios. 1. 21. 1. | Tree moss used in unguents w/ ben and ointments and analgesics | | |
| 1849 | Dios. 1. 22. 1. | Aloewood (eaglewood) alone or decoction | masticant | Mouthwash |
| 1850 | Dios. 1. 22. 1. | Aloewood | topical | Deodorant |
| 1851 | Dios. 1. 22. 1. | Aloewood (1 drachma) | drink | Excessive accumulation of stomach fluid, stomach limpness and heartburn |
| 1852 | Dios. 1. 22. 1. | Aloewood w/ water | drink | Pains in side and liver dysentery and colic |
| 1853 | Dios. 1. 23. 1. | Nascaphthon | fumigation | Constricted cervix (burnt bellow) |
| 1854 | Dios. 1. 24. 1. | Bisabol (3 obols) w/ water or vinegar and honey | drink | Thins obese people |
| 1855 | Dios. 1. 24. 1. | Bisabol | | Splenetics, epileptics and asthmatics |
| 1856 | Dios. 1. 24. 1. | Bisabol w/ hydromel | drink | Brings on menses |
| 1857 | Dios. 1. 24. 1. | Bisabol | | Removes scars from the eyes |
| 1858 | Dios. 1. 24. 1. | Bisabol w/ wine | | Dim sightedness |
| 1859 | Dios. 1. 24. 1. | Bisabol | | Pyorrhea and toothache |
| 1860 | Dios. 1. 25. 1. | Cyphi | oral | Antidotes |
| 1861 | Dios. 1. 25. 1. | Cyphi | drink | Asthmatics |
| 1862 | Dios. 1. 25. | Recipe for cyphi | | |

| | | | | |
|---|---|---|---|---|
| 1863 | Dios. 1. 26. 2. | Saffron adulterated w/ chopped saffron residuum and litharge or galena and daubed w/ must | | adulterant |
| 1864 | Dios. 1. 26. 2. | Saffron | general properties | Digestive, emollient, astringent and diuretic properties |
| 1865 | Dios. 1. 26. 2. | Saffron | oral | Healthy complexion |
| 1866 | Dios. 1. 26. 2. | Saffron w/ grape syrup | drink | Counters nausea |
| 1867 | Dios. 1. 26. 2. | Saffron w/ woman's milk | topical | Stops tearing of the eyes |
| 1868 | Dios. 1. 26. 3. | Saffron | drink | Internal afflictions |
| 1869 | Dios. 1. 26. 3. | Saffron | suppository or poultices | Uterine or rectal afflictions |
| 1870 | Dios. 1. 26. 3. | Saffron | oral | Aphrodisiac |
| 1871 | Dios. 1. 26. 3. | Saffron | topical | Inflammation from erysipelas |
| 1872 | Dios. 1. 26. 3. | Saffron | topical | Ear inflammation |
| 1873 | Dios. 1. 26. 3. | Saffron (3 drachmae) w/ water | drink | Poisonous dose |
| 1874 | Dios. 1. 26. 3. | Saffron root w/ grape syrup | drink | Diuretic |
| 1875 | Dios. 1. 27. 1. | Saffron residuum (remains after making saffron unguent) | | Removes cataracts, diuretic, emollient aids digestion and warms |
| 1876 | Dios. 1. 28. 2. | Elecampane root decoction | drink | Causes urination and menstruation |
| 1877 | Dios. 1. 28. 2. | Elecampane root w/ honey | lozenge | Coughs, orthopnea, ruptures, spasms, flatulence and animal bites |
| 1878 | Dios. 1. 28. 2. | Elecampane leaves boiled in wine | plaster | Hip diseases |
| 1879 | Dios. 1. 28. 2. | Elecampane root preserved in grape syrup | oral | Stomach |
| 1880 | Dios. 1. 29. 1. | Egyptian elecampane single root w/ wine | drink | Help those bitten by animals |
| 1881 | Dios. 1. 30. 1. | Young olive oil | drink | Good for the stomach |
| 1882 | Dios. 1. 30. 1. | Young olive oil (held in the mouth) | masticant | Staunches the gums and firms teeth |
| 1883 | Dios. 1. 30. 1. | Young olive oil | topical | Antiperspirant |
| 1884 | Dios. 1. 30. 1. | All oils | topical | Warm and soften flesh |

| | | | | |
|---|---|---|---|---|
| 1885 | Dios. 1. 30. 2. | Olive oil | drink | Ease and soften bowel and take edge off abrasive medications |
| 1886 | Dios. 1. 30. 2. | Olive oil (drunk and vomited) | drink, purge | Poisons |
| 1887 | Dios. 1. 30. 2. | Olive oil (1 cotyle) w/ water or barley water (eq.) | drink | Purge |
| 1888 | Dios. 1. 30. 2. | Olive oil (6 cyathi) boiled w/ rue (drink warm) | drink | Colic |
| 1889 | Dios. 1. 30. 2. | Olive oil (6 cyathi) boiled w/ rue | drink | Intestinal worms |
| 1890 | Dios. 1. 30. 2. | Olive oil (6 cyathi) boiled w/ rue | enema | Intestinal obstruction |
| 1891 | Dios. 1. 30. 2. | Old oil | topical | Warms more, aids perspiration |
| 1892 | Dios. 1. 30. 2. | Old oil | salve | Sharp sightedness |
| 1893 | Dios. 1. 30. 2. | Wild olive oil | topical | Headaches |
| 1894 | Dios. 1. 30. 2. | Wild olive oil | topical | Stops perspiration and the falling of hair |
| 1895 | Dios. 1. 30. 2. | Wild olive oil | topical | Clears dandruff, scurf, mange and leprosy |
| 1896 | Dios. 1. 30. 2. | Wild olive oil | topical | Delays hair greying |

Milton Keynes UK
Ingram Content Group UK Ltd.
UKHW010649250923
429338UK00001B/134